French Toast

Colin MacArthur

Published by Second Leg Publishing, January 2019
ISBN: 9781775366010

Typeset: Greg Salisbury
Proof Reader: Lee Robinson
Book Cover Design: Judith Mazari

I dedicate this book to Chrissy and to all of the Chrissys out there. To the Sarahs, and Pennys, and Debras, and Trevors, and all those who suffered abuse at the hands of another. Especially those who suffered abuse as a child. If I could give you back the childhood you deserved, I gladly would.

Acknowledgements

I would like to thank all of my beta readers and editors who did so much to make this into a readable book, especially Bernice Lever, Lena Armstrong and Dee MacCarthy. Without their help, I would never have achieved a publishable story.

1

"I think she fancies you," said Rob.

We were headed back to the hospital's Microbiology Lab from our lunch break. Rob was the Chief Technician, and I was an unqualified dog's body, preparing cultural media for the testing of specimens and responsible for the autoclaving and safe disposable of those specimens after testing was complete.

"I think it is you she fancies," I said.

"I'm married," Rob protested.

"Yes, and so?" I replied.

"I think that you should ask her out," Rob concluded, as I swung open the door to the lab, and he breezed on past me to disappear into his office.

Those of us who were either too lazy, too forgetful or otherwise disorganised and therefore without lunch to eat, often gathered in the "Coffee Shop", a collection of basic tables and chairs, randomly placed in the Second World War Nissen Hut. A short wall of red bricks on two sides covered with a curved, corrugated metal roof. Windows poked out through the roof along the side of the building. A double door at one end and a curtained stage at the other, attesting to its previous incarnation as the entertainment centre of the hospital.

The hospital itself, with its lead-paned windows and flat roof, was a rambling collection of red brick wards, either side of the long undulating corridor. It had all been built in a rush by the American troops stationed in England during the war. Built for those of its soldiers lucky enough to have made it back across the channel, but unlucky enough to have been wounded or become sick during their time in Europe. As the last soldiers headed for home at the end of the war, the locals took over. Some thirty years later, it was still being used as one of the local hospitals and looking very much like it had the day the Americans left. But it had become a respected teaching hospital, full of doctors in training and more importantly, student nurses.

The 'she' that Rob referred to was just such a student nurse. Christine was eighteen and had arrived about a month previously as one of the latest batch of student nurses. Half a dozen people could come and go from the Coffee Shop, and no one would notice. Christine stepped through the door, and the whole pace of the place changed. I looked up to see this tall, slim gazelle, looking around the room. As part of their initial orientation to the hospital, Rob had shown this year's intake of nurses around our lab. That was enough to lead some of them to join us at our table. Luckily, Christine, seeing a vaguely familiar face or two, came and sat down. We made her feel welcome.

Now on days when we were there, she would join our table, whether there were any of her fellow student nurses with us or not. But as for showing any specific interest in any of us, I couldn't say.

"Ask her out," Rob had suggested. That was easy for him to say. Oh, it wasn't so much the fear of rejection that slowed me down. It was more the fear of total embarrassment if my invite should be entirely unexpected or somehow felt to be inappropriate. I was thirty years old. It was usual for me to flirt to the point where my intentions were clear and only then if the flirting was returned, would I venture forth with an invite.

However, that was not always possible. Sometimes there would be a window of opportunity, a brief chance that might never come again. Now, this could be one of those times. A first date should be memorable, but that wasn't always possible in this town. The pub, the cinema, maybe a restaurant, if you had some money to shell out. In this case, there was to be a hospital barbeque in about a week's time; this was something that had never occurred before to my knowledge.

The girl I had been seeing was leaving town, on a locum for two weeks. I had no idea why we were dating each other, and even if there was no one to take her place; our dates weren't going anywhere. We hadn't talked about having an exclusive relationship. In fact, we hadn't talked about the relationship at all. I didn't feel sorry, therefore, when finding Christine sitting alone a few days later, I summoned up my courage and asked her if she would like to go to the barbeque with me.

"If my boyfriend doesn't come down at the weekend, I will."

I tried not to show any reaction to those words: if my boyfriend doesn't come down. Never in any of the conversations at our coffee table had a boyfriend been mentioned. A jolt of electricity poked me in the ribs, but I used my poker face and said, "OK, just let me know, and I will get the tickets." Then I walked back to work, half of me floating on a cloud, the other half dragging along in the gutter.

2

The boyfriend didn't materialise so on a Friday night in August, we waited with a growing group of hospital staff - boyfriends, girlfriends, even some married couples - until right on time, a big green double-decker bus rolled around the corner and stopped in front of us. We piled on, upstairs and down, with a palpable air of excitement, a noisy babble of voices filling the bus.

One of Christine's fellow nursing students called out, "Hi, Chrissy," as she passed us on her way to her seat. Christine didn't respond.

"Was that you she was saying hello to?" I asked.

"I don't answer to that name," Christine said sternly. "I do not answer to any shortened version of Christine. You have been warned," she added and then her mood lightened again.

The weather was being kind to us, blue skies and warm

evening air without being uncomfortably hot. The bus was more suitable for a run around town than a twenty-five-mile jog through the country, but nobody was complaining. The stage was set for an adventure, and few of us knew quite what to expect, least of all me.

No one took too much notice as this big green bus rolled through town. It was a common sight after all. Every second person was talking, and that left Christine and I to talk about our personal histories. How we came to be working at that hospital. Our likes and dislikes, all without fear of our fellow passengers overhearing.

I asked why she hadn't chosen a hospital closer to her hometown, and she told me she didn't want anywhere too close to her parents. That was not a surprise from a teenager moving away from home and wanting some freedom, so I hadn't questioned it further. Not that any more details would be forthcoming even if I had. But we talked easily, and both listened intently, so we filled the time without feeling ill at ease.

Nearer our destination, we were passing through villages where a big green bus was a less common sight. The few locals out walking would sometimes stop and stare, and our busload of revellers would react wildly. Excitement grew until finally, we were rolling across the beach, then for sure, everyone stopped with puzzled expressions on their faces. Double-decker buses did not drive across sandy beaches, but there we were, soon tumbling off of the bus onto the sand. We were all eager to see what the evening had in store for us.

I was looking to spend the whole of the evening with Christine, but the event organisers had other plans. The girls went off to play rounders somewhere out of sight, and the boys split up into two teams for a manic game of soccer. All of us dressed in summer street clothes with sandals or trainers or whatever we had happened to wear. None of us dressed for the game, and with sixteen or more players on each side, it was difficult to tell who was who: teammate or foe. Then after the first goal was scored through the make-do goal post, the teams began to be a little lopsided. There was a tendency to want to be on the winning team.

I merely wished to survive the game. Perhaps even look as if I was putting in the effort, but with no wish to be carried off to the hospital. At one point, I ran for the ball, up against one of the youngest players there. No problem I thought, barely a teenager. Bang, it was like running into a brick wall. After that, I made sure that I survived intact, ready for the barbeque that I knew was waiting for us.

So finally, we were back queuing, paper plates in hand for our hamburger, green salad, potato salad and pop in a paper cup. It tasted like a feast after all that running around. Christine was quiet after the game, but we found a beautiful place on the sand, in front of a recently lit bonfire. What little breeze there was carried the smoke away from us as we ate our dinner. The light had started to fade, but the evening air was still pleasantly warm.

As I finished my food, I leant back on my arm, stretched out behind Christine's back, ever hopeful that she might lean back against me. But she stayed sitting bolt upright with her beautiful posture as somewhere just in front of us the first strains of guitar music filled the air. A male nurse who had joined us for the trip filled the air with those familiar words, "And they were singing, Bye bye Miss American Pie." For the next thirty or forty minutes, he entertained us with the popular songs of that era. Until finally in the growing darkness and with an almost full sky of stars, he sang "Starry, Starry Night."

It was beautiful and romantic, and somehow better than I could have hoped to arrange for a first date, but at the same time, it wasn't really feeling much like a date at all. Sadly, that happens, she had told me she had a boyfriend. Oh, what a night he had missed. He had been invited; I wondered what had kept him away. It was a bit of a drive, and it was Friday night, so perhaps he was working and couldn't get away on time.

3

Finally, there we were back at the hospital, tumbling off the bus, scattering every which way. I wasn't sure what to expect. I walked Christine back toward the nurses' home, a carbon copy of the rest of the hospital, but separate and set back almost in front of our lab. I was aware of one young nurse, Sue, who I had had a brief fling with. She was following along the path with her girlfriends, so I was hoping I would be invited in for coffee.

Christine and I made small talk as we neared the front door of the nurses' home, and I dearly wanted to slow my pace to avoid an awkward goodnight. But I could feel these eyes staring at the back of my head. I desperately wanted to speed my pace so there wouldn't be an unwelcome comment if Sue decided she needed to make a snide remark.

"Would you like to come in for coffee?" Christine asked just as we were nearing the door.

"Yes, that would be nice," I replied. "Although I shouldn't stay too late, I have to work a half day at the lab in the morning." I was relieved to be led down the corridor to the back of the nurses' home and into Christine's room.

It might have been a nun's cell, small and barren, white painted bricks. A single bed against the wall under the window. It had a wardrobe, chest of drawers and a nightstand. A sink hung on the wall with a small mirror above it. Christine had tried to make her room more personable: a few pictures, a poster on the wall, her table light on the nightstand. She had her own electric kettle that was soon boiling for our coffee. Nearby she had her record player along with a small collection of LPs.

We sat on the side of her bed and thumbed through her records, discovering I had, at least, three of them myself. "Play something that you like," I said. "This is my chance to hear something new."

So, coffee in hand, we sat and listened and talked easily again for a while. It was strangely comfortable; Christine seemed relaxed again, and we were chatting like old friends. We shared our tastes in music and books and contrasts we had in our families, our personal histories. Christine finished her coffee and pushed her pillows up against the wall, sitting back relaxed.

The coffee in my hand, I was sipping slowly, trying to make the moment last. Dreading when I would run out of coffee and time. Twice in the last week or so, this woman had taken me out of my comfort zone. If I try and kiss her, I may get my face slapped and be sent out the door. If I don't try, I have run out of time, and I am going to be out the door anyway, perhaps never to have another chance. And so, hoping that she couldn't hear my heart pounding in my chest, I lent forward placing my now empty coffee cup on her nightstand and turned leaning in towards her.

"No, please don't," she said. "My life is very complicated at the moment, and that would only make it worse." I turned back facing away from her.

"Is it something you would like to talk about?" I asked. There was no answer for a while, but I sat there quietly, having had some experience in letting people talk their troubles out.

"I think I might be pregnant," Christine stated with a resigned air.

"I see. Does the father know?"

"Yes, he says he loves me and that he wants to have children with me one day. But he thinks that we are too young. He says that I have just started my nursing career and that he is still trying to establish himself. So, we can't afford to have kids right now."

"And you," I asked, "what do you think; what do you feel?"

"He is right, of course, we can't do this right now. It would ruin everything."

I wanted to glance around; I wanted to see how she was coping and not just try to guess from the sound of her voice. But I didn't want her to feel she was being judged. I wanted to let her be as comfortable in this situation as possible.

"What about your parents, do they know?"

"No," Christine stated very firmly, "and you must promise me right now, that you will never tell them."

"OK, I won't tell them." At that point, I wasn't expecting ever to meet them.

"No, I need you to promise me right now. Promise me."

I looked over my shoulder towards Christine; there was a look of utter panic on her face.

"I promise you that I will never tell your parents." I watched as her face relaxed a little. "So, what is the plan?" I asked

"Mike is going to come up with the money, and I'm going to have an abortion." She paused. "There is no other choice."

"But you don't know for sure yet, do you?"

"I'm pretty certain, but no, I haven't had the test yet. I have to take my urine sample to the lab in the morning." Her voice tapered off.

We sat quietly for a while; I was glad that it wasn't the lab that I worked at that was responsible for her pregnancy test. I was at a loss to know what to say. I would like to have given her hope. I would like to have been able to put some sort of positive spin on things. But there was nothing.

"A couple of weeks from now I will have a long weekend leave. There is a hospital in the next county where I can get it done." She must have heard my question, even though I hadn't asked it. "I don't want anyone here to know about it. It's hard enough without having to deal with that."

"When will you find out, for sure? When will you get the results?"

"Monday evening. I have an appointment with my doctor."

I glanced over towards her. "Dr Brennan," she added. "Now can we change the subject?"

So, we did. It was very late, but I wasn't going anywhere after that. I knew I could survive my four-hour shift in the morning, even on no sleep. Every four weeks it was my turn to cover the lab and do the rounds of the local hospitals, picking up specimens and dropping off reports. It was a simple routine task.

"I need to get some rest," Christine announced after a while. "Would you mind turning your back for a minute while I get into bed?"

I stood and turned away from Christine and the only mirror in the room until Christine was climbing into bed.

"Okay," she said, and I returned and sat briefly on the edge of the bed.

"Would you like me to meet you outside of your doctor's office on Monday evening?" I asked. "I'll be almost passing the door on my way home."

'That would be good, thank you." she said, adding that I could lie on the bed beside her.

"Thanks, but if I lie down I'll be asleep in no time, and I would never make it into work. So, I'll sit here on the floor until it is time for me to leave. You get some sleep, and I'll be waiting for you when you get out of your doctor's office on Monday." I gave her hand a brief squeeze and sat quietly on the floor for the next hour or so, and then I let myself out.

The following morning, work passed quickly enough, as I knew it would, and with nothing much planned for that weekend I caught up on my sleep. Christine crossed my mind, once or twice, but it wasn't a problem I could solve. Perhaps I could offer her a little support and help her deal with it, but the decision was made. I was little more than a bystander, an observer at an unfortunate time in a single lady's life.

4

I was earning just over the minimum wage right through the nineteen seventies. Hospital staff were underpaid, and the unqualified support staff even more so. It was a great job, worthwhile and fulfilling. I got to work with the best people: intelligent, interesting, caring people. I had enjoyed the tail end of the hippie era, and money was not the most important thing in our lives. We had better things on our minds, and I didn't always notice the lack of cash in my pocket.

I rented a flat. It was referred to as semi-furnished. What this meant was that those articles of furniture that previous tenants had left behind, I could use. If it wasn't there, I would have to supply it myself or do without. The carpets were threadbare; the wallpaper was dated and peeling. There was a gas stove that may have been state of the art twenty or more years before I got there, but it worked. As did the fridge, small but large enough for a single person. The freezer compartment would hold a bag of peas and a small box of fish fingers. If I wanted ice cubes, I would have to eat either the peas or the fish fingers. Then there would be room for the ice tray.

The rent was probably reasonable at the time, but being single and in a lower wage bracket, I was able to apply for and get a housing allowance from the county. I took in my pay slips and my rent receipt, and I received a small rent allowance. Nothing fancy but I could survive. Never did they suggest I take in a flatmate or find somewhere cheaper. I had experienced sharing with a flatmate, and that wasn't good. As for finding somewhere cheaper, I think that, at that time, I was lucky to have found anywhere at all.

The best thing that could be said about the place was that it was mine, mine to come home to, to lock the door and shut out the outside world when I wanted to. It was big; the top floor could have been four bedrooms. Or as it was; one bedroom, one make-do darkroom, a studio room for me to shoot pictures and an empty room that a model might use to get changed. It was also within walking distance of the hospital, perhaps thirty minutes, for the months, the years, when I couldn't afford to keep a car on the road.

On the downside. It didn't have running hot water, without carrying wood and coal up from the backyard, lighting a fire and nursing it along for an hour or so. It had single pane sash windows some of which would almost fill the openings they were designed for. The ceilings were twelve feet high, and as heat rises, the ceiling might be warm in winter, but the rest of the room would often be lacking warmth. The living room did have a fireplace, and sometimes I would have a nice fire burning, but, for the most part, I would use a portable electric fire or a paraffin stove. Often moving them from room to room as needed. In places, the floor didn't quite meet the wall; this was most noticeable in the living room where you could peer down through to the flower shop below.

The bathroom I cheerfully referred to as my wind tunnel. The window didn't fit very well, and the door never sat squarely in the door jam. It was long enough to be two rooms in any modern house, but this was no modern house. It was a "town house." Not what you would call a townhouse now, but back when it was built for a well-to-do family, this was the house that they would use when they came to town. They had their country residence and their town house. One could still see the fittings where the pull cords and push button had been that they used to call for a servant.

I was so glad to have my own place. To call it basic would be generous for its many shortcomings, but it was what I had and what I could call home.

5

As promised, Monday evening found me waiting outside of Christine's doctor's office. I didn't have long to wait, and I didn't have to wait for her to tell me the results. It was written on her face. Her chin was down; the weight of the world was pulling on her shoulders. As I walked up to meet her, she nodded a resigned acceptance of her news.

"I'm sorry," I offered. "I had hoped for a better outcome, for you."

"Thanks." Christine's voice was barely audible.

"I live just up the road from here. Would you like to come for coffee and perhaps sit and talk, if you feel up to it?" I asked.

"Yes, please," was all the response she could muster.

She walked quietly along; I described the route and the distance and anything else that I could think to say, but more because I needed to take the sting out of the moment. Finally, I was opening the big back gate and leading Christine through the mess of retail cast-offs. In through the back door, past the buckets of flowers that lined the hallway and up the flight of stairs. It was a momentary distraction for Christine as she took in the riot of colour and fragrance of two dozen or more varieties of blooms.

We sat in my kitchen as I made us both a cup of coffee. Christine asked how I came to be living above a florist shop, and she told me how she had noticed the shop in passing when her nurses training sessions had taken her to the other hospital. For now, her days were mainly in the classroom but with occasional trips to various wards, mostly for orientation and background information on the source of a nurse's duties.

Then we moved into the living room; Christine didn't seem to notice the ragtag nature of my place. If she had, she was too polite to say anything. She thumbed through my record collection, noting our similar taste in music. We played some music and talked about whatever we thought might be on television that evening and generally just avoided the topic of her pregnancy. She seemed to be content just to have my company and to know that I was there should she feel the need to talk.

"I know that you may not feel very hungry," I stated, "but I am going to need to eat soon. I will make enough for both of us, and you can eat as much as you can manage. Just make yourself at home here, and I will start some food. If you feel the need to join me, come on in."

My definition of poor at that time was not being able to feed an unexpected guest. So I usually had something at hand, although I didn't often have a call to feed anyone. But here it was needed. At the time, you could get cannelloni prepared and ready to heat in a tinfoil package. It kept well just sitting on the pantry shelf. I had bought it, ever the optimist. One day I might have company for dinner. I opened a tin of sweet corn and boiled some potatoes that I mashed with milk and a little butter.

Christine surprised me, eating more than I would have expected, but when I commented on the fact that she had done well, I got the obvious answer. "It's better than hospital food." So, I left her to search for something on TV, as I cleaned up in the kitchen. Soon we were both sat on my loveseat with its stretch cover, watching one of the three available channels on my old black and white set.

We were comfortable; it was easy to talk, and it was just as comfortable seated side by side saying nothing. Once or twice the subject of her current situation came up; it was discussed briefly and then we were distracted by something on the television. I made some more coffee. I was happy just having her there with me until I noticed the evening was slipping away. I didn't want to say anything, but the hospital was a half-hour walk away, and we both had to work in the morning. Or rather I had work, while Christine had a class to attend.

"Do you mind if I don't go home tonight," Christine asked. "I don't feel like being on my own right now."

"No, I don't mind, come on upstairs." My bedroom was as basic as the rest of my flat. A double bed that was two old double mattresses on top of each other on the floor, an old fashioned dressing table and a wardrobe. "Here," I said, after a little fishing around in a drawer. "You take the tops, and I will wear the bottoms." I handed Christine the top half of a pair of yellow pyjamas with brown piping. They were rayon, but they looked and felt better than they really were. They had almost never been worn.

Then I excused myself and went down to the bathroom to change and get myself ready, leaving Christine to change and climb into bed. I returned and climbed in beside her, and we both laid on our backs side by side. I reached out my left hand, and Christine held it. We talked until slowly the gaps in the conversation took over, and we both drifted off to sleep.

6

The next evening, I stopped by Christine's room after work as arranged. We had coffee together and walked across to the hospital cafeteria to have some dinner. Soon we were back in her room, and she was thumbing through her record collection.

"Do you mind if we just go back to your place," she asked. "I don't want to be here right now."

"Come on, let's go," I said with a wave of my hand towards the door.

Christine picked up her handbag, threw it over her shoulder, and we walked out of the nurses' home and headed toward town. So, for a second night, we watched a little TV, and we laid in bed side by side, holding each other's hand and talking. It just seemed a natural arrangement, and if this is what it was going to take to get her through her troubled times, well yes, I enjoyed being with her.

The next day when she was due to be at the hospital at my end of town, I gave her my keys. Now she could let herself in if she had finished before I got home. It was a long time since I had been in such a close relationship, so even though I was going to have to let her go soon, I could enjoy it in the meantime.

Christine would stop by her room in the nurses' home, pick up a change of clothes, check to see if there were any message to say that her boyfriend had called. There was always a nurse waiting for a call from someone. So there was always someone to answer the phone and take a message because they would all want to know that somebody would do the same for them. Then she would meet up with me or just go on over to my place on days when I was already home.

We would eat together and hang out, and then lie in bed, wearing our respective halves of my pyjamas and talk about the past, the present and our hopes for the future. Often it was late, well into the night before we would run out of things to say or otherwise just become too tired to talk and drift off to sleep.

Then it was Friday and the weekend in front of us. It seems very strange to me now because I shower every day, but that was 1978, and my flat didn't have a shower. Heck, it didn't even have running hot water. True most places would have hot water, but there weren't that many showers around, and people wouldn't necessarily wash anything more than their hands and face every day. Yes, I might have a strip wash at the sink if I had gotten hot and sweaty. If I had had to work hard, I would boil a kettle of water on the stove, then freshen up at the sink.

But Friday, Friday was usually my bath night, and Christine had not spent any extra time at the nurses' home where they had showers and running hot water. So, at dinner, I explained my routine, and she said, "Yes, a bath would be nice." So, before

I had even cleaned up from our meal, I went down to the backyard and carried up the coal and some kindling to get the pot-bellied stove going. It would take an hour even in August to produce enough hot water to fill a bath. Then, try as I might, I could never keep the stove running well enough to have extra water to top up the bath as it cooled down.

So, it took a considerable amount of time, but finally, I was able to announce, "Your bath awaits, my lady. I will let you go and get in so you can have your bath first. Would you like a cup of coffee to enjoy while you soak?"

"Yes, please," Christine answered.

"I already have the kettle on; it won't take long," I told her, as I returned to the kitchen. Not only did I have the kettle on, but I also had every saucepan that I owned full of water and heating on the stove. I knew that the water tank would never reheat in time to warm up the bath as it cooled. I knew too that I would often drag myself reluctantly from the bath as the water became too cool to stay there. So tonight, the plan was to let Christine take her bath, then I would warm her leftover water as best I could and take a bath myself.

With her coffee in hand, I headed out to give it to her, not quite sure where I would find her. I peeked around the door into the living room, but she was gone from there. "I have your coffee here," I ventured at a half-opened bathroom door.

"Thank you," Christine replied from where she was already soaking in the hot water.

I had thought to hand it to her as she headed toward the bathroom door, instead, here I was standing beside her as she sat in my full-length cast iron bathtub. My pulse quickened as I tried to make the situation as normal as possible. "There you go," I said handing her a mug of coffee, "I'll leave you to have a soak."

"You are going to have a bath too, aren't you?" she asked, only half glancing up at me.

"Yes, sure I am," I replied with a little question in my voice. "Well, you might as well climb in here behind me."

I wasn't expecting that. "I'll be right back, I have to turn the water off on the stove." The pots were boiling by now, and I turned off the gas. I popped up to the bedroom and quickly changed into my dressing gown, and then I returned; my coffee in hand to join her in the bathtub. I climbed into the bath behind her and carefully slid one leg on either side of her. I leant back and tried to act relaxed. We sat with my legs resting on hers and her back just a few inches in front of me, drinking our coffee and talking. A perfectly normal Friday evening. No, but that would be nice, in the future. A shared bath, with some quality personal time together. I was getting used to having Christine in my life far too fast.

"You can wash my back if you like," Christine said.

I should be getting used to her surprising me by now. But I wasn't. I did, however, pick up the soap and lathering up my hands, proceeded to wash from her shoulders down to below the water line. Then I rinsed the soap from her back and stopped.

"Is that it?" she asked.

"You want more?" And so I lathered up and did it all again, this time making it less about washing her back and more about a relaxing contact, a shared moment. "There, how was that? I asked.

"Once more," was her answer.

And so I did, enjoying the firm, fine-boned structure of her back. All the while trying not to show how sexually interested in this tall, slim body I had become. Wasn't I supposed to be her support group? Her one-person cavalry, coming to her rescue.

Then with a "Thank you," she leant back against my chest and finished her, by now, very cool coffee. I laid my left arm on top of her left arm. We sat like that a while, till the water was noticeably cooler. "Now I had better go and let you finish up," she added and grabbing a towel, as discretely as she could, she stood and wrapped the towel around herself and was gone.

I still had some hot water on the stove, and I was tempted to warm the water but maybe next time, if ever there was a next time. So, I soaped my body and rinsed it off as well as you can in the bathtub. Then I dried myself and went upstairs, put on my pyjama bottoms, cast off my dressing gown and laid down next to Christine. Lying hand in hand and talking for a while before falling asleep.

7

By now it will be no surprise that I was never a man's man! I grew up with a mother and three sisters and a stepfather who had the answer to every question that had ever been asked as well as many a question that hadn't been asked. His reference to the females of the human race as "stupid cows" left me thinking that there had to be a better way to live. Especially, since I had always been interested in these delightful creatures for as long as I could remember.

Soon now, Christine would be gone. She had arranged a lift from a friend, someone from out of town that was to pick her up from her nurses' quarters and drop her at the hospital where she was to have her op. Then her boyfriend was to be there to visit her when it was all over, and a day later he was to pick her up and drive her back to town. At which point I had to expect to be out of the picture.

But then a couple of nights later as we were lying in bed, our usual routine, Christine suddenly asked, "Are you gay or something?"

"No, I'm not gay," I said somewhat surprised.

"Only I have been here about ten days or so, and you haven't even made a pass at me."

"I didn't think that was what you needed right now," I said.

But then rolling over towards her, with the slightest of pauses, I kissed Christine firmly on the mouth, my hands on the buttons of her pyjama top. I delighted in every touch, every curve, every caress. With both halves of the pyjamas discarded on the floor, we made love for the first time. The whole world disappeared, even the walls of the bedroom; everything slipped from my consciousness, except the few cubic feet that we occupied.

When I fell back exhausted and so very ready to sleep, Christine said, "You know if you were anything of a lover you would go down and make me some French toast now."

"French toast," I had to ask. "Whatever is this French toast?"

"It is easy," she replied, "just beat a couple of eggs in a bowl, coat both sides of a piece of bread and fry it in your frying pan. Medium heat," she added. "Oh, and some salt and pepper."

Soon I was in the kitchen, it didn't take long before I was returning with two slices of beautifully browned French toast.

"That looks great," Christine announced. "Where is yours? Oh, and I should have asked you to bring the salt with you."

"OK, I'll be back." As soon as I had the first slice of bread in the frying pan I popped up with the salt. Christine only had one slice left, and I knew I had better bring at least one extra slice for her if I was to get to eat some myself.

We sat in bed and finished up the toast. Then pushing the plates out of reach and turning off the table light, I kissed her on her salty lips. Rolling over onto my right side, I said, "Sleep well." With that, Christine turned over and forming us into two perfect spoons, she threw her arm around my waist, and we fell asleep.

The PJs would remain forever discarded, and for the next few nights, we slept locked together in a hug. When one of us turned over, the other would roll over too, and because we were the same height and close to the same size, we would lock together like a couple of jigsaw pieces.

Then all too soon it was time for Christine to go. "I have to stay in my room tonight and get myself ready for my hospital stay. I am getting picked up first thing in the morning," Christine told me.

"I don't know when visiting hours will be but would you like me to come and see you, Saturday afternoon?" I didn't know why I was asking this. Her boyfriend was going to be coming in to see her. He was to pick her up to bring her back on Sunday. I did not have a car, and this hospital was some twenty-five miles away. I would have to catch a train.

"That would be great," Christine said, and I knew that she meant it. "As long as you discreetly excuse yourself, if you are there when my boyfriend arrives."

"Of course," I really didn't think that I wanted to meet her boyfriend, but I had already decided that I would be there for her. I knew that she was having a really tough time with all of this, and if I could be of any support, then at least I could do that much for her.

8

I really can't recall the details of our conversations, nor the order that things fell into. I was always open and honest with Christine. I told her about my past, my history, my hopes for the future and why not. I really had no hope of having a future with this woman. I had somehow stumbled across something wonderful; I had just had a taste of something I had never found before. However, my story.

I had been born into an idealistic life in a small town in western Canada. Mum, Dad, myself and three younger sisters. I had an uncle and aunt that spoiled me rotten, taking me away on trips, and having me over for weekends. I would help out in my uncle's TV repair shop, testing valves. I'm sure they were probably the same valves that I had tested for him a week or two before, and I typed some of the envelopes for the invoices my aunt was preparing. Then before I went home again, they would give me a dollar for all of my help.

In winter time, we had several feet of snow. We would build a snowman, have snowball fights, and one winter there was so much snow I built a fort. A big tall wall with a shelf sticking out that I could walk along. If it broke, I would fall laughing into the piles of snow below me. We would take our sleigh, the four of us, and walk a few streets over to the hill that started at the back of our local park. When it started to become too dark to see very much, we knew that it was time to head home. It was only when we walked in the door that we would realise we were becoming cold. Then as the warm smells of dinner hit our noses, we would realise that we had also become famished.

In the summer, I would hop on my bike and ride off, exploring the park behind us or cycling down the riverside to visit my uncle. No bicycle lock yet never any worry about whether it would still be there when you went to pick it up. If you become thirsty, you would take a drink from the river or a garden hose. Get hungry, help yourself to a carrot from the garden. We would run through the sprinkler on the front lawn or make a tent out of a blanket to make some shade to keep ourselves cool. Mum would bring us out iced lemonade as a refreshing treat.

Sometimes we would picnic on the lawn, sometimes the whole family would gather, uncles and aunts and cousins. I was eleven heading on twelve, living in an endless summer, except it was not endless. My father became very ill, then this tall giant of a man wasted away. Between long stays in the hospital and trips home to be with his family the innocence of our youth started to disappear. Then he passed away, and although we had never had a care in the world, everything changed.

I was told that I was the man of the family now, to look after my mother and my sisters. What did that mean? I wasn't even capable of looking after myself.

We weren't taken to the service or even taken to stand at his graveside. I am not sure that was the right decision, but that was the one that was made for us. We had a family hug, the five of us, a few tears, and that was it. Very soon afterwards Mum called us together to ask, "How would you kids like to go to England to live?"

"Yeah," a bunch of excited sisters replied.

"So, would you like to fly there or go by train and boat?"

"Train and boat," a chorus of my sisters' voices replied.

With that, it was decided, although I'm reasonably sure the decision was made long before the question was asked.

So, I was twelve years old, and there we were in England. How terribly strange everything was. The school year had already started, but the first thing they did was to sit me down to take something called the 'Eleven plus'. You should have taken this a year ago, they were telling me. I wasn't here a year ago, and a month ago I had never even heard of pounds, shillings, and pence. How many fluid ounces in a pint, or what is a quart again? Needless to say, I failed miserably, so they decided to tuck me away in this new school that had only just opened. I was the third oldest pupil in this school that only had grades one and two, except what was this grade two business? I would have been going into grade seven back in Canada.

It wasn't going to matter too much because I would soon have a stepfather whose advice to me was, "Don't waste your time with education, go out and get yourself a real job." Which translated to "You are one too many mouths to feed, I really don't need you around!" Then he told me how wonderful it would be for me to be in the armed forces and how much he loved it when he was in the navy. "You can learn a trade, then you would be in big demand when you get out."

So, at fifteen years and two months of age, I was signed up and in boot camp. I went from living with a mother and sisters to living in a navy mess with dozens of other males. Kit inspections, marches, a discipline that seemed to have no rhyme nor reason to it. Yes, I learnt a trade, electronics, but when I got out four plus years later, no one in Civvy Street had the first clue as to what my qualifications meant. Love it, no. I hated everything except the electronics. Travel none; I was stationed in the south of the country, I never went anywhere.

After the services, I tried retail for a few years with some success, then as a short order cook in a fast food chain with less success. Long hours with little job satisfaction. When you should be out enjoying the evening or home watching television, I was behind the counter rushing to fill food orders. Then dumb luck or coincidence landed me a job in the hospital service, and that is where Christine came into my life.

But there were two other things that I had told Christine. Along the way. I had been married before for about twenty months. This didn't bother her at all, nor at the time did finding out that I was nearly twelve years older than she was. She had no plans to keep me. In fact, she had no plans for me at all.

9

Saturday morning, I walked to the railway station to catch the train. The plan was to spend a few hours sitting with Christine, then catch the next train home. I arrived in good time and found the hospital quickly enough, not too far from the train station, so I walked around waiting for visiting hours to start. I was wondering what I would find, whether I would get to spend much time with her at all. I half feared I would arrive to find her boyfriend already there or that he would show up soon after I got there. Then I would have wasted my time and money.

Finally, I walked into the ward to find Christine sitting up in bed, somewhat subdued, but happy to see me. After asking how she was, and how she was feeling, I ask if she had seen anything of Mike. No, she hadn't seen him, nor had she heard anything from him since she got there. "He will probably wait until this evening before he drops by," she said, but I detected a note of uncertainty in her voice.

"How are you going to get back, if he doesn't show up to give you a lift?" I asked.

"I don't know," she admitted, "I don't think that they will discharge me unless there is somebody there to look after me."

"I could find a cheap B&B and stay over just in case," I offered.

"Would you mind?" she asked.

"No," I told her, "I will come back this evening to let you know what is happening, and we will see if he shows."

With that, we sat, and we chatted about this and that; the time quickly passed until I took off to find somewhere to stay the night. I didn't have to go too far. Many places around the hospital were cheap and cheerful. I found myself a toothbrush, some toothpaste and a meal, before going back for the evening visiting hours. Still, no sign of the boyfriend, so I was glad that I had offered to stay. In the morning, there was a light breakfast at the B&B. I checked out just about as late as I could. I strolled around the neighbourhood until finally, I thought it would be time enough to show up at the hospital.

I was still earlier than the suggested time for my arriving, but Christine was sitting dressed, ready to go. Her face brightened as I walked through the door. "Doctors rounds are over, and I am free to go," she announced. I picked up her little overnight bag of the few things that she had with her, and we headed out the door.

Outside the hospital was a taxi stand, where we grabbed a taxi to take us to the railway station. It was a short trip, and usually, we would have walked or taken a bus, but I had no idea how Christine's energy reserves were, so we took a cab. At the station, I purchased two first class tickets, the only way I could be sure that she would have a seat. I didn't want to take a chance on her having to stand the whole way. Then when we arrived back in our hometown, we took another taxi. As the driver pulled away, I asked Christine, "Where do you want to go?"

"Let's go back to your place," she replied, so I called out my address. There we were, much to my surprise, back in my flat. We didn't talk much about what had just happened; we didn't talk much about her boyfriend not showing up. I cooked some dinner; we watched television, and that night I held her in my arms as we fell asleep. In fact, for the next several nights I just held her.

But soon we settled back into a relationship again. Christine checked her mail slot every day while she was at the hospital, and she checked her room to see if she'd had a phone call. There was nothing for several weeks. I began to think that was the last of him, then out of the blue, a phone message. A note on her door told her that Mike had called and that he would try to call again tomorrow.

"I have to be there to see what he has to say for himself," declared Christine. "Will you come up and wait with me?" she asked.

So, we went to her room after work and waited. We were sat listening to her music when a fellow nurse knocked on her door. "Phone call for you," a voice rang out.

Christine was gone for about ten minutes and when she returned I couldn't tell what to make of her expression. She plonked herself down on the bed, looking across at me.

"He didn't show up because he landed himself a good job, on some farm, and they wanted him to start right away. He has moved into a flat above their garage; it doesn't have a phone, but there is one in the farmhouse. However, it is a bit of a walk for the farmer to come and fetch him. So I'm only to phone in an emergency. He told me he missed me, and he promised to call on a regular basis."

"What does that mean," I asked.

"I told him that I was not going to sit in here every night waiting, on the off chance that he will call. So he agreed he will call me Wednesday at eight, and that he would work out a time that would work for both of us on the weekends."

"And you want to be here for that?" I asked.

"Yes, I guess, I'll see what he has to say for himself, I suppose that I should stay here, shouldn't I?"

I wanted to tell her she should dump him, but I kept quiet.

"I would really like it if you would drop by for coffee after work." She wasn't quite sure whether to look at me or not. "We could watch some TV or just hang out here."

"I'll see you soon," I told her, and I hugged her tight to my body, then headed home alone.

10

Christine's early life sounded as if it should have been ideal, although she seemed to be vague with some of the details. She had grown up in a stately home, a grand old estate that had been handed over to the care of the country. Her father was the gardener, and they lived in a flat above the stables that were now the garages. Her mother didn't work, but she did volunteer sometimes when the house was open to the public.

The house had vast gardens, both formal and fancy as well as a significant natural area of countryside stretching out in front of the house. It had its own small lake, its own church which was set between the village and the gardens. The church was open to the villagers for the service held every Sunday morning.

Just about an hour before the service was due to start,

Christine's father would open the church. He would wind the century-old clock, then ring the tower's single bell. Home for Sunday breakfast and then back in time to ring the bell again with fifteen minutes, ten minutes and then five minutes to go; calling the faithful to the Sunday morning service.

Christine and her mother would join him at the church; they would take their place in the front pew where the vicar would beam down on them during his sermon. The villagers would comment, "What a lovely family they make." Then they would be sure to heap praise on the vicar at the end of the service, telling him how much they had enjoyed his sermon. They were always last to leave as her father would lock the church before they headed off for the rest of their Sunday routine.

Their flat looked out over their own large garden where they produced much of their own food. There were a tool shed and a woodshed. Part of the stream that fed the lake ran through their garden. The wages of a gardener were not significant. They didn't reflect the workload, but it did include their rent, so between their frugal lifestyle and the food they grew for themselves, they managed to get by.

The village had a small elementary school; the local kids could walk to class. A few others would arrive by car, but that was it. A small village that couldn't even boast a Post Office or store. Every purchase meant a trip to the next village or a longer trip to town, but there was no longer a bus service. The locals relied on each other for those times it was necessary to make a purchase or visit a doctor.

A mobile library would visit the village every other week. Then there was a van that came around with bread and milk, plus a few essential supplies. That was it; they were isolated from the world in their small community with quiet routine daily lives. The biggest noise was the call of the peacocks, an occasional car passing through the village, or maybe a distant aeroplane.

11

I had been single for a good many years now. Girls came and went from my life, and it wasn't a big deal. My marriage had been a naive mistake. How quickly my every thought had come under the microscope, and since then nobody had given me the feeling that things could be different.

But something did feel different this time, perhaps because I wasn't being chased. I didn't feel that, after just three dates, my whole life was being planned out for me. Christine had no plans for me at all, and I had no real hopes for a future with her. Yet it felt so very comfortable being together.

I began finding myself meeting Christine after work. We'd have coffee together in her room, eat hospital canteen food for dinner and then sit together watching television in the nurses' lounge. Or sometimes we'd listen to music in her room and play a game of Turncoat. I had never heard of it before, but she had brought it from home and was glad to introduce me to it. The occasional walk was pleasant; she seemed to find freedom in the fresh air on warm evenings. In a garden or in a park, away from the hospital, I could almost imagine her flirting with me.

Then it was Wednesday, Christine left me in the TV room just before eight and headed down to the phone booth, just inside the main entrance of the nurses' home. Mike was right on time; they chatted for about ten minutes, then Christine returned to join me in front of the television.

That was our life. We spend most days together, like close friends. Saturday, I came out to meet her as arranged, Mike had just phoned, right on time again I noted.

"Now that is over, I'm free to wander off," Christine said. "Let's go window shopping."

Neither of us had much money to spend, but we could

explore the shops, discovering more about each other's taste. We didn't dare go back to my place; it didn't even get a mention, but Christine was glad to be outside and away from the hospital for a few hours.

Christine hadn't actually made any girlfriends in the few months she had been a student nurse, and I didn't think to question that. I didn't make male friends easily, so maybe it just felt normal for these things to take time. But it was good to be with her, and even though I wanted to reach out to take her hand, I had to settle for enjoying the time I had with her.

Come Wednesday she was gone for quite a bit longer than she was the week before. I was thinking that they were finding more to talk about, but no, when Christine returned she told me he had been a bit late calling. She had little to say about the conversation, and I began to get the idea that most of the talk was about him, about what he was doing.

"Let's go and take in a movie tomorrow," I suggested, "my treat."

There was no phone call that weekend, nor was there a call on Wednesday. I tried to offer reasons why he might not have been able to call. It was hard to think that he couldn't have gotten through and left a message sometime during the week or so, since his last call. I was hoping that was the last of him, but I was telling Christine, "Give him a day or two."

"He can't expect me to sit here waiting for him," she said. "Let's go home, to your place."

So that is what we did. We were a couple again, and although Christine checked for mail and messages every day, there was no word from him to explain his disappearance from her life.

12

"Feel free to pitch in and help out around here," I told Christine. Up until this point, she had been my guest, and I had cooked and cleaned, but - as I told her - if she was going to stay, it was time we shared the chores. That was it; we both did whatever it was that needed doing after which we were free to spend more time together. However, when she needed to study, I left her to her books, and I took over the chores. It worked well; study or do chores, the trade-off helped her get her books out a bit more often.

Life was good. We shared our hopes and dreams; we lived and acted like a couple, but we hadn't actually started to talk about being a couple. We would lie in bed and talk late into the night, especially when we were first back together and on the weekends. Friday night we would fire up the old pot-bellied stove and then about eight o'clock, when the water was good and hot, we would run a bath. I would get every pot I owned full of water and heat it all to boiling point, then turn off the gas before we would climb into the bath.

I would wash Christine's back countless times, then when she had enough of that, I would wrap my arms around her, and we would lay back in the water. When it started to cool, I would ask her if she was ready for a coffee then I would get out, rush back to the kitchen and bring the water back to a boil. Then in I would go with each saucepan, in turn, pouring in hot water while Christine stirred. Finally, I would bring in our coffee. Climbing in behind her, we would resume our conversation or just enjoy the warmth of the water.

When we weren't talking until we were tired and ready to sleep, we were making love. It flowed without inhibitions. It felt warm and tender and, for me, it was a sheer delight. Then, of course, there was French toast. I had learned my lesson; now I would bring up a large plate of the stuff, along with the salt shaker.

Over time, I had shared the best of my photography with her. A few commercial shoots but mainly fashion, glamour and some nudes. I only ever showed my best work, reasonable but not great. Still, I was improving. Christine wasn't bothered at all by the idea of me photographing other women, and she seemed to appreciate my pictures. It was refreshing to have someone in my life that was supportive of my creative efforts.

I had already sat her down in my make-do studio, trying to capture on film the way I felt about her. I always fell short, and as usual, the model is her own biggest critic. But some evenings when the mood took her she would ask, "Do you have any film in your camera?" We would be heading up to the bedroom, and I would fetch one of my flashes on a light stand. Christine would pose coyly on the bed, exploring her sensual side, and when she felt more confident, well, she was beguiling.

It was always an attempt to be artistic but knowing that I was the one processing my own film, that didn't hurt at all. It was foreplay. It was intimate. It was part of the sheer joy of being together. I could have lived in that moment forever.

13

Soon it would be Christine's nineteenth birthday, and I was wondering what I could do to make it special for her. As always there was not much extra money to throw around. Maybe a steak dinner at home, a night out at the movies. This would be my first time for buying her a present, and I wanted to do it right. She wasn't expecting anything much; she knew I was just getting by, but it was a chance for me to say how much I cared for her.

Christine came home from work one evening announcing that she had received a letter from Mike. I had put him out of my mind. I had become so acclimatised to our living together, and this threw me through a loop. "What does he have to say?" I asked.

"He wants to see me, he says," Christine replied. "He says he has a surprise for me."

"After all this time, does he say why he hasn't been in touch?" I asked.

"No, he wants to get together for my birthday. I have to go and see what this is all about," she added. "I'm sure that you were trying to plan something for my birthday. I'm sorry."

I wanted to tell her not to go, that she was crazy to give him the time of day, but it wasn't going to do me any good. I could see that she still had feelings for him. I could see that she was secretly excited at the thought of seeing him. She was subduing any excitement for my benefit, and I kicked myself for wanting to be with her so much.

We didn't talk like we usually did; we didn't say much. She held me tight to her body, and we slept like two spoons in a drawer. Turning over every now and then but always in close contact throughout the night. I didn't want to know what the plans were. In fact, Christine didn't know the plans at that point, as Mike was to phone the next evening and make arrangements.

Christine went back to her room in the nurses' home, waiting for his call. I was at home alone for the first time in months. Tomorrow I planned to drop by after work and visit for a while; it was several days yet before the weekend, but I was going to have to step back and leave her to explore her possibilities. Reluctantly I told her to enjoy her weekend, that I would see her Monday evening. It was going to be a long few days.

Monday arrived as it always does; I was distracted at work thinking about Christine. After work, I took the short walk over to her room and knocked on her door. She quickly opened it and stepping back announced, "Good news. Oh, I guess it is not good news for you," she said, very briefly deflated. Then she bounced right back. "Mike and I are engaged." She flashed her new ring at me.

Now I'm no expert on rings, but it looked more than reasonable for a nineteen-year-old. Maybe a fifth to a quarter of a carat, in a lovely gold setting. She was more than a little pleased with herself.

I offered my congratulations, accepting her offer of coffee. As we sat on her bed, she told me details of her weekend. Why he said he hadn't been able to stay in touch and how his job had gone so well they had given him a pay rise. Oh, how he wanted to do things differently this time and what a great meal they had at this lovely restaurant, and how excited her parents were for them both. All of this in a jumbled rush of words. All I could do was to smile at appropriate moments in the dialogue and listen.

"I was thinking," she said. "Well, it won't be fair to him for me to stay living at your place. Would it be all right if I drop by after work tomorrow and pick up my things?"

"Yes sure," I answered, "I'll be home at the usual time. I will see you tomorrow," I added before excusing myself.

14

Christine arrived as expected; she didn't have that much stuff at my place. I made coffee as she ran around collecting up her bits and pieces. It all fit into a canvas carrier bag, and she was soon back with me in the kitchen.

"Well I am excited for you," I offered. It was a half-truth at best.

"Thank you," she said. "Here, you had better have your key back."

I motioned for her to put it on the table, reluctant to be taking it back. "Do you have everything?" I ask, searching for something to say.

She merely nodded, then giving me a brief hug she was gone.

The place seemed huge all of a sudden, I was left to rattle around trying to find my bearings. Hoping she had overlooked something and that she would be back looking for it or that I might have an excuse to deliver it back to her room. I found nothing, and I whittled away the evening in front of the television.

At bedtime, I saw her toothbrush sitting with mine, in a glass on the sink, and it caused me to smile. A small part of her was staying behind with me.

It was going to take some adjusting. It had only been a few months, but everything had seemed to fit together so well, for me. I wasn't sure why; perhaps it was just a case of me being old enough to be ready for a commitment.

Work meant walking past the front door of the nurses' home every day. Heading to work, I hardly noticed it but going home in the evening, that was a bit tougher. It had been an unlikely pairing all along. So little chance of it going this far. But it had awoken a dream in me.

Three days had passed with me watching the door of the nurses' home out of the corner of my eye as I walked past. It was inevitable that I would see her at some time; the hospital wasn't that big. It was a surprise, however, to see her coming out of the doorway on the fourth evening.

"Hello," she said, uncertain as to what sort of reaction she was going to get from me.

"Hi. How are you doing?" I ask, with a slightly surprised but pleasant tone to my voice.

"I would still like to be friends with you," she ventured. "You could still come by for coffee, or we could hang out sometimes. I know it is not the same, but I would still like to see you occasionally."

"I'll stop by after work tomorrow, and we can talk." I offered.

"OK that would be nice, I'll be here," she told me.

I continued my walk home, slightly elated as Christine turned and headed back inside. Perhaps there is some sort of an outside chance. I didn't really notice at the time, but I used to be so good at letting go.

Coffee and music in Christine's room, then hospital food in the canteen followed by a few hours in front of the television with a small group of the other nurses and all for a good-night hug. A half-hour walk home alone in the dark, the evenings were cooling; it was midway through October.

I wasn't there every night, but it got to be more and more frequent as we began to talk again, enjoying each other's company. I began to realise that Mike wasn't calling. He wasn't getting a mention in our conversations. We might take in a movie or share a daytime walk on the weekend. Nothing too exciting, then one Friday evening a couple of weeks into this new arrangement Christine asked, "Why didn't you bring your camera with you?"

I was a little puzzled, "I don't usually carry my camera around with me," I told her. It was getting late, and there hadn't been much on the television, so we were back in her room, listening to her records.

"I feel like posing for you," she said. "Why don't you go home and get your camera?" she added. "It will be worth it."

"It is half-an-hour's walk each way, you won't still be in the mood when I get back," I told her.

"Yes, I will, I promise. I know. Why don't you take my bike, so you can be home and back in no time? Come on, let's go and get it." Christine led me down the corridor to the bike lock up.

I was reluctant. Actually, I was sceptical. But I cycled off into the dark, to collect my camera, some film and my flash gun, and headed back as quickly as I could. True to her word she was still up and waiting for me. The clothes she had worn were now replaced with a dressing gown, and the music was softer and more romantic in nature.

She was a little coy at first, but then she slowly peeled the dressing gown from her shoulders, undoing the buttons as I took shots of her posing in her easy chair. "Turn the light off," she suggested. "Then I won't be so timid."

"I won't be able to see to focus," I told her. "I know, I will sit here and focus on you, and you go and turn the light off. Let me know when you are ready."

They were not the most artistic shots I have ever taken, but Christine gave a huge part of herself to me that evening. It didn't hurt that she knew that I processed my own film, but even so, it was a statement of trust. A moment of vulnerability, a moment, where she opened herself to me, I truly treasure that gift. I cherish the pictures, but even more than that, I treasure that moment with her.

A few days later as we sat sharing a coffee in her room, I looked across at her and said, "He isn't phoning you, is he?"

"No," she said looking down and then with a brief pause she added, "Let's go home."

15

Little by little, Christine moved more of her things back to my flat. We started to develop a life together, small hints of a social structure. She kept her room at the hospital, and she still checked for mail and phone messages, but Mike never called again.

We were sharing chores around the flat, even our trips to the public laundromat. We hadn't had to plan these things or discuss how we should do the household chores, we just pitched in and got them done. Christine took more interest in how the flat looked, we bought some paint and a few cork tiles, and although the place was beyond hope, we did what we could to make it more home-like.

The living room had a small ledge at about eight feet from the floor, above that was about four feet of wall and the ceiling. It was painted a colour that was once white. Over the years of coal fires in the grate, not all of the smoke made it out of the chimney. The white was now a soot grey. We decided to paint that last four feet and the ceiling chocolate brown. It made the room looked wider than it was tall.

In fact, it was so successful that about a week later I arrived home from work to find that some of the bright orange wallpaper in the kitchen was now brown. I never did like that orange anyway, but I hadn't intended to paint the whole place. But it did look better when it was done, even if it was a little dark.

At this time I was working Monday to Friday with the rare Saturday morning thrown in. Christine was training five days a week, but they could be any five days. Usually two consecutive days off but not always. We had our evenings together, but now we had some time for ourselves to pursue our own hobbies and interests.

Photography was always my hobby and preferably photography in which a model was involved. I would have loved to turn it into a business. I had made an effort to drum up some work from local businesses, with limited success. Usually, I would photograph something for them and make just about enough to cover my expenses.

I photographed windows for a glazing company, wicker chairs for a furniture importer, but they had very limited appeal to me. Then I met Jeff and his Dance Apparel and Clothing Company. He was always glad to have new items of clothing photographed, and he would find models from girls that wandered into his shop. I would get some worthwhile pictures to add to my portfolio as well as having my costs covered. But the real bonus was some of the models that he sent my way.

One such model was Sandy, a tall, slim, dark-haired beauty. Flaky and unreliable but a total delight to photograph. After some successful pictures of her in the latest leotards, leggings and jumpsuits, I had suggested that her body would be well suited to doing some figure studies.

"Oh, sure that would be good," she replied, and so it was

arranged that we would do a shoot starting at noon on Saturday. This would give me four hours of shooting time, and I could still tidy up in time to be starting dinner when Christine got home. Except Sandy didn't show up at noon, nor one o'clock, in fact, it was closer to three.

She was sorry, something had come up, but she still wanted to do the shoot. So, we started soon after three and the next couple of hours flew by. I had, of course, told Christine about the shoot and hinted at some of the details, but I had expected to be finished and to show her the best of the pictures a week or so later. As discreetly as possible, as it wasn't something that had endeared me to many of my old flames.

Then there was a knock at the studio door. "Would you two like coffee?" Christine asked.

I looked across at Sandy, who nodded. "Sure, that would be great," I replied.

Soon after Christine arrived back knocking on the door, so I called, "Come on in."

Christine walked in with a tray and three mugs of coffee. Sandy had picked up a towel, which she held in front of herself, to hide her naked body.

"This one is yours," Christine announced standing directly in front of Sandy and Sandy lifted the mug from the tray. Then she turned to me with a smile, and I took my mug from her tray, with a thank you. "I'll see you guys later," she added and then she was gone.

"I would like to have stayed and watched you work," she told me later. "But then I thought that it might have inhibited Sandy, especially when she wasn't expecting me.

And so, not for the first time, I thought, Christine is a keeper.

16

We had talked about our hopes and dreams as individuals, our pasts, present, and futures but never had we talked about our relationship. Christine hadn't planned to have a relationship with me, and as for myself, it was just some kind of beautiful pipe dream.

Then a new conversation started. One day Christine said, "I wish you were younger," as we were walking towards the hospital.

"I wish you were older," I replied. "If I were much younger I would not have coped with everything we have been through."

"I still wish that you were closer to my age," she continued. "I would trade you four years if I could give you four years, so you are four years younger, and I am four years older. That would be perfect."

I never felt my age, and I had not considered the age gap when I had asked Christine out. Nor had I asked her out with any kind of long-term relationship in mind. She was strikingly attractive; more than one head was turned when she walked into the coffee shop in those early days at the hospital. More than one set of eyes followed her as she crossed the room, trying to be discreet while their girlfriend was distracted.

I had been less than successful in my long-term relationships. I was at the point where I didn't think it would ever happen to me, but then I had never been so close to actually being ready for a commitment.

Even so, we were a long way away from a commitment, but we were starting to talk about our relationship. Besides which, we were starting to socialise as a couple.

So, one evening Christine came home and told me that her friend Eve was going to the movies with a boyfriend. "How would we like to join them?" she asked. "Make up a foursome." They both worked at the hospital, and so I knew them in passing.

"Sure," I said, "sounds great. What is the film?"

"A Star is Born, with Barbra Streisand." I didn't know much about the film, but I had listened many times to Christine's voice as she sang along with Barbra, and I was impressed. More so because I couldn't carry a tune myself for more than two notes in a row. We both loved music, rock and pop and even a little classical from time to time. And yes, it would be great to get out for a change.

We sat there engrossed in the film, hand in hand. I was already enjoying the moment for what it was, but then Christine turned to me and said, "I love you." It was unexpected, out of the blue. She wasn't looking for a reply; she simply turned back to the film. I gave her hand a little squeeze and smiled to myself. The love word had never come up before, although I'm not sure why, but after I kissed her goodnight I told her, "I've always loved you."

17

It's Christmas; the town centre is being decorated, and the shops are full of seasonal gifts. The festive spirit is starting to spread. Christine had already arranged that she would be home for her four-day Christmas break, but in the meantime, we could start to create our own Christmas traditions.

A young woman who had modelled for me sent me an invite to a 'bring your own bottle party'. It was an easy walk from my place, so we picked up a bottle of wine and headed over. Neither of us knew many of the other guests, but we mingled and enjoyed the finger food. More than one younger guy found a reason to talk with Christine although she always wandered back to my side before too long. Music had been playing ever since we arrived and as the evening wore on some of the furniture was pushed aside; soon people started to dance.

"Would you like to dance," I asked Christine.

"Sure," she replied, and we mixed in with the rest of the dancers.

"You didn't tell me you could dance," she shouted in my ear.

"I've had a little practice," I replied.

So, we danced a while, then we rejoined the party in the kitchen, drank some more wine, chatted and snacked. Then danced some more. The music had started to slow down, and I held Christine in my arms as we pivoted in gentle circles.

"I think that you should take me home," Christine whispered in my ear. "When I feel like this you can do anything you like."

We made our brief thank-yous to the host and headed home. I had never seen Christine inebriated before. Not drunk just pleasantly high. Home wasn't far, and we were soon there, Christine squeezing my hand all the way. I let her use the bathroom first, "I'll be right up," I told her as she headed for the stairs, and I was as quick as I could be.

A few minutes later I was in the bedroom undressing, but Christine was fast asleep. I smiled to myself as I slid into the bed beside her. There would be many more nights to share.

The next day we were decorating our place with a small Christmas tree we had bought. A few Christmas cards on the shelves, some holly on the mantelpiece. A bit of mistletoe, and a couple of Christmas candles, while Christmas songs played on the stereo.

We planned our Christmas dinner for a few days before her trip home. The smallest turkey we could find, but we both agreed, we had to have a turkey. Mashed potatoes and cranberry sauce with Brussels sprouts and gravy.

"Christmas pudding with clotted cream for dessert," I insisted.

"Mandarin oranges," Christine added. "Oh, and pork pies for Christmas Eve, we have to do that."

18

What a difference four days can make. Christine had been excited about our Christmas, she was bubbly and outgoing. She was as content as I had ever seen her. She seemed to be enjoying life, and now she was telling me that she was going to move back to her room.

"I need to study," she declared. "We have our first real exams coming up soon."

"You can't study here?" I asked.

"It is just a distraction; I need to move forward," she said.

She was not very forthcoming about her Christmas trip home. I know that she had taken each of her parents a nicely wrapped gift, but when I asked what she had been given, she was evasive.

"I just got some new clothes," she said, then she quickly changed the subject.

I hadn't seen this coming; we had been so close, but she was packing up a bag and getting ready to call a taxi. I had thought that these days were over when Mike disappeared.

"Did you tell your parents about Mike," I asked. "How he treated you?"

"I told them a bit. Obviously, I couldn't go into details. I told them what I could. They liked Mike. They thought that he was great for me. They didn't want to hear that he dumped me. They thought that I must have been out running around so he couldn't get a hold of me when he phoned.

"They didn't believe that I was there every night," she added with a quiet, resigned air.

"'He bought you a ring like that and then just dumped you, without a word' my mum said with disbelief, then she added, 'I can't understand why he would do that! Do you?'

"And no, I didn't understand either." Christine was talking

to the floor at this point, and I couldn't process this information fast enough to have any sensible answers or questions.

"Did you tell them about me?" I asked.

"I told them I was seeing someone new," she told me, "I didn't go into too much detail."

Then she was gone, with no arrangements to meet up at all. There was no "I'll see you around." She was gone. Her key was on the table. My head was spinning. I wanted to check every drawer and cupboard for some sign of her, but I didn't. I just walked into the bathroom, and her toothbrush was still there with mine in the glass.

Somehow that mattered, somehow that was reassuring. There was a small part of her staying behind with me. This little ray of hope looking up at me first thing every morning and last thing at night.

19

"Chrissy, take the dog for a walk. Go right up to the top garden and don't come home until I call you."

"Who are those people Mommy?" the confused six-year-old asked.

"Do as you are told and don't ask stupid questions. Now go." Mrs Wilson thrust the dog's lead into her daughter's hand and pushed her out the door.

"Come on Brandy, we can go for a nice walk. I don't think I've done anything wrong, Brandy."

Brandy was an adorable golden brown and white cocker spaniel. He didn't understand much of what was said to him, but walks and dinner, he had those two down pat. Yet he seemed to understand Chrissy's need to talk. That was one thing he was good at: he could sit and listen.

They walked to the very top section of the garden, then they walked around the path. On each circuit, as they were heading toward the flat, Chrissy would carefully glance towards the windows. "I don't think that anyone is watching us, come on Brandy, one more time around."

Chrissy didn't want anyone to know about her secret place in the woodshed. Under an old discarded table in the corner of the shed, she would crawl in and sit hidden, talking her troubles out as Brandy would sit and listen to every word.

People almost never arrived, and if they did, it was usually just that one sweet old lady. Chrissy liked her; she smiled and said nice things to her. She always made her feel good, but these people; they just rushed in and didn't even notice her.

"I think there is trouble Brandy, Mommy and Daddy are shouting again."

By the time the call to return came, Chrissy almost missed it. She had long stopped talking to Brandy, and for Brandy, that was a sign that it was time for him to go over and lay his head in her lap. She had closed her eyes and allowed herself a chance to relax.

"Why don't you come when you are called," her mum boomed as Chrissy finally approached the doorway. "Dinner is ready. Put that lead away."

As Chrissy entered the kitchen and climbed up into her chair, she noticed there were three place settings. The high chair was missing. "Where are Marty and Sarah?"

"They are gone. Now no more questions."

"But Sarah is my friend. We play after dinner." Chrissy pleaded.

"Enough, it is over; they have a new home now." Then sharply, sensing another question. "Stop right now. No more foster kids, no more."

"We were going to start school together after this summer." Chrissy sobbed, and a lonely tear made its way down her cheek. I'm not to cry, I'm not to cry, she thought to herself, and she wiped it away with the back of her hand.

20

It took a while, but one day Christine was in front of me as I left the hospital coffee shop on a lunch break.

"Can you help me study?" she asked.

"Hi," I said with a half-smile, half-quizzical look on my face.

"I need someone to throw questions at me from my notebooks," she stated.

"I'll drop by after work," I offered.

"Thanks," she said as we both headed off back to our respective jobs.

The afternoon dragged on, but I went straight from work to her room. She gave me an extended hug, then looked sheepishly at the floor. "I have missed you," she said.

"I missed you too. So, are you ready to study?" I asked, "Or do you want to go across to the canteen and eat first?"

"If I have to eat one more hospital meal right now I am going to scream," she said with feeling. "Can we go home to your place?" she asked.

"It's bangers, mash and frozen peas," I warned.

"That sounds great, let me get some stuff together."

"Don't forget your books and your lecture notes," I added for good measure.

I wasn't a complete stranger to anatomy and physiology, having spent years in the hospital service, and I had been involved in a nurse's study period or two.

We headed home. There was a little talk of why she had left, although it wasn't totally clear, and I didn't push too hard for answers.

I had missed her more than I cared to admit, even to myself. I had become too attached to just walk away. Maybe she was just young and confused, maybe I was expecting too much from her. Maybe I was in way over my head already.

We made love and then we talked well into the night. Far too late for a work day, but we were young, and I knew that I could survive the next day just knowing she was back. The warmth of her body nestled against mine was dissolving the pain of separation. It was good, and I felt as if I was right back where I belonged.

We settled back into our routine, with a bit more studying than there was before. But we were once more a couple. Then something new happened. Something that I found difficult to understand and something that was a total surprise. Our sex lives had been open, relaxed and fulfilling. Then one night when I touched Christine's naked body, she tensed. She completely froze.

"What is wrong," I asked. There was no answer. "Come on, talk to me." Nothing.

She was in a near catatonic state; I could feel her fear, and I was utterly confused. This was not one of those 'I don't feel like it tonight' things. I was lost to know what to do, how to respond, how to help, how to cope. I couldn't get her to talk, and so I lay there confused and worried. At last, I rolled onto my side facing away from her and drifted off to sleep.

A while later her knees came up to mine, and her arm came across my body; we slept in our usual tight tangle of a knot. When one of us rolled over the other did too, and it was just like any other night.

This was just the start of a long period, sometimes easier than others, but never with the free and easy style that we had enjoyed in earlier times. I must admit that sometimes I became so frustrated, both sexually and emotionally, that I jumped out of bed, threw both hands down hard against the mattress and swore. I never swore, and so it was a very strong statement of what this was doing to me, then I would walk out of the room.

The fact that Christine was frozen in this catatonic state, unable to respond, just made it harder for me to cope. At first, I had thought that she was just about to leave, but if anything, we became closer together. Everywhere we walked hand in hand, then on the loveseat in front of the television, she sat wrapped in my arm. We slept in almost constant contact throughout the night.

But Christine could not talk about it. Not in the cold light of day and most certainly not while it was happening.

Neither of us ever forgot those three little words "I love you", and we never had cause to doubt them, but I was at a loss to know what was happening or what I could do to help. I was grateful for all the times that this issue didn't arise, and I lived in the constant hope that with time, it would pass.

21

Despite this new problem that we shared, things were good, and I was enjoying life. We were doing and sharing all of the things we had done before. Spring was showing signs of an early arrival so one bright sunny Sunday, we decided to head out for a walk. Christine was still fairly new to the area, so I suggested we walk out along the canal.

It was good just to be out in the fresh air, and I pointed out some of the places I had explored growing up in the area. After walking for a while, I pointed across to a council housing estate and told Christine, "This is where my parents live now."

Then on a whim, on the spur of the moment, I asked, "Would you like to drop in and meet them?"

"Sure, why not," she replied.

My parents had been in business and been reasonably successful, and then the recession hit. They had lost just about everything except the furniture they needed for living. Two fancy cars now became one basic run-around, but the stress was gone too, and so was most of the infighting. They were getting on better now than I had ever known them to.

I knocked on their back door, and we let ourselves in. "Hello," I said by way of announcing our presence.

"Oh hi," they replied. "Come on in."

"I want you to meet Christine," I told them. "We were just out for a walk, and I thought we would drop by."

"Excuse us while we eat," my mother said, but before the next mouthful she asked, "Have you had dinner?"

"No, we don't eat dinner until the evening," I told her.

"Well just let me finish this up. There is plenty, and I will fix you up a plate."

"We can get something later," I told her.

But she was cleaning up her plate and getting up from the table. "Come on in. Sit down," she beckoned. "I'll cook up a bit more veggies, it will just take a minute. There is lots of meat and potatoes." So we sat and talked, soon Mum placed a plate in front of each of us. Rabbit sections baked in seasoned bread crumbs, baked potatoes and vegetables.

"Do you play Canasta?" they were asking.

"What is that?" Christine asked.

"Stay a while; we will teach you. I'm sure you will catch on quickly," my mother added.

I had heard of it, but I had never played before. We cleared the table, and the rules of the game were explained. One dummy hand and then we were playing for real. Christine and I did well for novices and enjoyed the game.

The game itself took quite a while to play, and at the end of it, we were told how well we had done and asked, "Do you want to stay for another game?"

"We could play one more game, and then I will fix us some tea," my mum suggested. "And then we can drop you off, save you having to walk home."

So that is what we did, making a full afternoon of it. We played even better in the second game. Enjoyed a pleasant cup of tea and some family chit-chat, and then my stepfather drove us back to my flat. I smiled to myself because it was just assumed that we were living together. The only thing that had been said was that we didn't usually eat dinner until the evening, I guess that was enough.

"Wow, I can't believe your mother; she is amazing," Christine said as we waved goodbye to the car. "My mother wants two weeks' notice if I just wanted to bring a friend in for a cup of tea. She would have wanted to know exactly when we would arrive and when we would leave. Exactly what she was going to feed us and everything else down to the last detail."

We had an open invitation, to a home-cooked meal and a game or two of cards, anytime we wanted to stop by. "They like you," I told Christine.

22

"I really want you to meet my parents too," Christine was telling me some time later. "I will talk to them about it, so we can work out a time for a visit."

"OK," I said, uncertain as to what I was letting myself in for. "I guess I'll have to do it one of these days."

"They will like you; I know they will," Christine told me.

Then Christine proceeded to coach me on what to expect and how to behave, interspersed with reassurances that I'd be fine.

"You will have to sleep on the couch," she warned me. "Even though there are two single beds in my room and even with our living together, that would never do. They wouldn't let us share a bedroom unless we were married."

"What else?" she asked herself. "Right, they don't smoke, and they don't approve of my smoking, so if we want a cigarette, we will have to go for a walk well away from the house."

"That's fine," I offered. "No, problem."

"Then depending on the timing, well I don't think that we would have to go to church on Sunday morning." She sounded uncertain. "When I was a kid, we had to go every Sunday morning, but they don't have services there every week now."

"Mum will offer us a cup of tea when we arrive and usually half way through each afternoon. So that's fine," Christine continued, "but if she gets the biscuits out and passes them around, only ever take one. She might offer you a second one later, but just take one at a time. Oh, and whatever you do, do not dunk it."

I was beginning to think that I was being groomed to meet royalty or something.

"You'll be fine," Christine reassured me again. "You have good manners, and you're a nice guy, so don't worry about it."

"Don't worry about it," she said, but I could see that she was apprehensive. We hadn't even arranged anything yet.

Then she brightened, as she told me, "I can't wait to show you around the place. I don't know if the house will be open to the public, but we have full access to the formal gardens and the rest of the estate. We can take the dogs out for a walk, and oh, you will want to bring your camera. There are wild deer on the estate, and we may get close enough for some good shots."

"Then if the weather is nice, you are sure to get some great pictures of the formal gardens, with the house or the church in the background," she added for good measure.

23

Chrissy liked it best when it was just her and her dog, left to play on their own. Sunday was not her best day, but for some reason that afternoon they were left on their own in the living room. They played chase. Chrissy made a big fuss of Brandy and then she ran around in circles. Brandy loved to chase.

Around the room, in and out from behind the easy chairs.

Then around the coffee table and Chrissy would turn and chase Brandy, who wasn't quite sure what to do with this part of the game, so he was always far too easy to catch.

Suddenly as Brandy turned in one of his excited spins, his tail caught the teacup which sat on the corner of the coffee table. Over it went with a loud clatter, spilling the dregs into the saucer and onto the table, as it fell to the carpeted floor.

Chrissy was there in an instant. "It is all right Brandy; it didn't break," she said, reassuring herself more than the dog.

With that, the living room door flew open, and her mother suddenly appeared, just as Chrissy replaced the cup in the saucer.

"Why don't you look what you are doing?" her mother bellowed. "You careless girl."

"It wasn't me, Mum, Brandy knocked it over with his tail," Chrissy explained.

"Don't lie to me, you think I don't know what you get up to." Then with two quick steps, Mrs Wilson was there and swiped Chrissy across the head with the back of her hand.

There was a tear welling up in Chrissy's eye, from the shock and the pain as well as the confusion. She tried to hold it back as she said, "It was Brandy, honestly, it was."

"Get out of here," her mother demanded. "Go and play in the garden and I don't want to see or hear from you until your dinner is ready."

With that, Chrissy took the lead from behind the door and headed down the stairs.

"We will go to our special place, come on Brandy," Chrissy whispered bending to attach the lead to Brandy's collar. "Then no one will find us there. We will walk up into the garden, and when no one is watching, we will slip into our hiding place."

So, they walked to the top of the garden and back down again, several times, carefully checking the windows to see if anyone was watching. When Chrissy was sure it was safe, they slipped into the woodshed and under the table.

Only then did she let a few tears run down her cheeks. "It is all right Brandy; it's all right," she told him. "It wasn't your fault either. I don't blame you, besides it didn't even break."

"They are not my real parents," Chrissy continued. "One day my real parents are going to come back for me. You'll see, just like my foster sister and brother. But you know that. Someday soon they will come for me, and we will take you away with us too, Brandy. I promise we won't leave you behind."

24

Christine had told me, that the last time we were apart, she had booked herself a one-week riding holiday, in an attempt to cheer herself up and that it was all booked and paid for. And how she had planned to visit her parents for a couple of days at the end of her trip.

"Just stay safe and know that I will be missing you," I had told her.

That week arrived, and I saw her off at the bus station. It was all hugs and joy; she was sorry to be leaving me behind, but she was excited about her holiday. "Don't worry, I'll be fine," she told me. And off she went. It wasn't the horse riding that worried me. It wasn't the travel or the younger men. It was her parents, but then she had to be able to visit them and come away strong if we were ever to survive.

At home alone that night, I went to make myself some dinner. There was a love note in the fridge. I gathered up the things I needed and found another love note in the cutlery drawer. Then as I picked up my plate, there was another note, saying she missed me already.

It cheered me no end to find all of these notes, I did a search and piled them up together. And when I thought that

I had them all, I headed to bed. There, under my pillow was the sweetest note of all, saying how much she missed being there in bed with me. "I will be home soon, Love Christine."

As the week passed I received a postcard from Exmoor, saying she was enjoying being able to ride each day, the weather was being kind but oh, how she missed me.

The week passed quickly enough, and I was looking forward to being with her again on Monday evening. When Christine arrived, she announced that she was leaving me. Yes, she had enjoyed a good weekend home with her parents and no, it was not just them.

"What about these?" I asked, waving her pile of love notes in front of her.

"I'm sorry, I," she said, tapering off. Not sure what to say for herself.

I was mad, and I let her know it. I raised my voice, and I said things I didn't mean and shouldn't have said. I knew that it was all about her parents, and I had no idea how to solve the problem.

Christine left, and I was home alone. For how long this time, I wondered. I don't think it had ever been more than two weeks that we had been apart since that first date, and this was the longest continuous period that we had spent together.

As the week went on, and I hadn't heard from her or seen her anywhere, I decided to make a small statement of love. I bought a current love song that was being played on the radio that sounded appropriate. Then without a note, or even anything to say that it was from me, I slipped into the nurses' home and left it hanging on the door to her room.

I walked past the entrance to the nurses' quarters every evening as I left work, with a heavy heart. No sign of her, but one evening as I left the hospital grounds, she was there, heading up the street towards me.

"Thank you for the record," she greeted me. "I just had to get away and think about things for a while. Can we try again?"

I didn't have to say anything. I turned around beside her, took her hand, and we walked back to the hospital together.

25

Soon, we were back to our old selves, and growing closer together all the time. We ate, slept, worked, and played together. Christine studied, and I helped if I could. We had long soaks in the bath; only now we had an old fashioned washtub, the type with a big wringer on the top. We would plug that in and boil up the water. When it was ready, we wheeled it into the bathroom and emptied it out into the bath. But we would still have to boil up all of the saucepans on the stove so we could warm up the bath as it cooled down.

Christine would model for me. I had cobbled together a couple of "studio lights", basic battery powered flashguns on old tripods, and a couple of white umbrellas I had picked up at a camera "Buy and Sell." I still had no way of measuring what the exposure should be. I would measure the flash to subject distance with a tape measure, do some arithmetic, and then in my darkroom, clip off a piece of the film to do a test process. Then when these few negatives were dry, I would decide whether I needed more or less processing time.

After years of photography, I had perhaps four reasonable prints that I was pleased to show anyone who was interested. And for some reason that escapes me now, I decided to take those pictures to the newly opened theatre in town and ask to have a photographic exhibition in their reception area.

"Yes, sure," he said. "Let me see." Then he gave me dates right then on the spot. I was to have the whole of the coffee shop, for a one-man exhibition, for one full month. I was elated as I headed home to tell Christine, then it struck me. Whatever am I going to show? I don't have enough work to fill that room. And he needed a print soon so they can put together a poster to advertise the show.

Christine was very supportive, it meant long nights in the darkroom, doing the printing, putting together my makeshift frames and spending every available penny on this exhibition.

In the meantime, life went on. Our sex problem would still rear its ugly head from time to time, only now I had a name for it. Rightly or wrongly, I thought that the trouble stemmed from the fact that Christine's parents didn't want us together. They hadn't even met me yet, so I worried: would I ever get them to accept me? Perhaps then the problem would fade away.

However, even with the problems, life was good. We had very little money, and Christine was forced to keep her room in the nurses' home. One more expense we could have done without. That was her postal address, and that was how her parents contacted her. A letter now and then. They didn't have a telephone. Everyone had a telephone except Christine's parents, but perhaps that was a good thing. They were only ever going to call in an emergency, and Christine wouldn't get the message until the next day.

I was starting to feel my lack of income. The only time that I had noticed it before Christine was when I did my weekly grocery shopping. I had stood in the supermarket debating whether to buy this large bag of no-name chicken nuggets. If I could live on chicken nuggets or fish fingers all week, then I could afford to buy a roll or two of film. There was just room in the freezer for one bag of something.

Now I had this very special woman in my life, and I was beginning to notice the things that we couldn't do. And I really wanted Christine to stay this time. Perhaps a little side trip, a day out. I had been paying down my credit card as best

I could after having spent all of that money on my exhibition, so there was a little room for an unplanned expense.

"How would you like to take a day trip this Saturday?" I asked her. "There is somewhere that I would like to take you."

"Where are we going?" Christine asked.

"You will have to wait and see," I told her. "But it is south, and it is out along the coast."

On Saturday, we took the train out through Somerset and down to the south coast of Devon. Along to Cockington, a place I had discovered when I had worked briefly in that area. From the train, there was a short walk along the front before we arrived at the point where we could either walk on up the road to the village itself or ride a horse-drawn carriage.

We opted for the carriage ride along what was little more than a country lane. High hedges either side with just the occasional view of farmers' fields as we passed by a gateway. So even though we were seated much higher than we would be in a car, you still didn't see too much.

We arrived at the village. It was like stepping back in time several hundred years. There before us was a fully functioning blacksmith shop. A fire burning and a blacksmith in period costume hammering on a red-hot piece of metal, making a horseshoe right there on the anvil. A quick glance at the other visitors would reassure us that we were still in the modern era.

The Barber Shop had all of the tools of the trade out on display, and we found out a barber would also do double duty as the local dentist. Maybe even as a doctor at a push. Oh, how times had changed, and I was glad to think that my hairdresser stuck to cutting hair.

A house contained the latest refinements of the period. A hand pump to draw water, and a large metal tub that one might sit in front of the hearth on bath night. We thought that our flat was basic. With their outside privy and no running water, you had to wonder how they ever made it through the winter.

We had lunch in the village's café. It's one concession to the modern world. Electric lights displaying their selection of food and refrigeration cooling the pop, even ice cubes on demand. We enjoyed our hot soup and fresh bread, and a very welcomed coffee before heading out again.

Next to the village, they had extensive gardens surrounding a lake. Manicured and well kept, with pathways to explore the grounds. Christine was in her element here, naming flowers and talking about growing seasons. She was just generally relaxed and glowing, and I knew it was worth every penny to see her like this.

We wandered every path, and we even walked through the woodland on the edge of the property before we reluctantly decided it was time to head for home.

26

"Doubtless they thought they would have a bit of an adventure," the constable was telling Mrs Wilson. "No harm was done."

"Thank you so much, officer," Mrs Wilson said, with a sweet demeanour written all over her face.

A concerned driver had pulled off of the highway and found the nearest telephone, to call the police. "There are two young girls walking across the Severn Bridge, heading towards Wales."

"By young, what do you mean?" the police officer asks.

"They seemed to be carrying school satchels, and I would think that they couldn't be much more than twelve or thirteen. I think that someone should go and check on them. It is a school day, I'm sure."

"Thank you, sir, I will send a car out there right away."

It was the last thing Chrissy had been expecting, she hadn't reckoned with this. But suddenly there was a police car with flashing lights pulling up beside them. The officer was kindly, but firm. "Where are you young ladies from?"

"Churchly, sir," a crestfallen Chrissy answered.

"Come on, climb in, your adventure is over for today," the officer stated, pleasantly.

Mrs Wilson's attitude changed in an instant with the closing of the door. "Whatever do you think you were doing," her mum bellowed, "bringing shame on the family like that?" as she grabbed Chrissy by the hair and pulled her head down sharply, thrashing her with hard, fast blows to the buttocks and the tops of her legs.

Chrissy spun trying to get away from the pain, but it only tightened her mother's grip on her hair, and the slaps kept coming. Finally, her mum threw her down on the settee, and Chrissy's hands came up instinctively to protect her face.

"Get to your bedroom and don't come out until you are told." Her mum yelled, "There will be more to come when your father gets home!"

Chrissy threw herself on her bed, wrapping her arms around her pillow and burying her face. She cried a large damp patch on the pillow. Sure that no one would see, she cried until the tears wouldn't run anymore, but still, she clung hard to her pillow. Fearful of the moment she knew was inevitable. The moment when the turning of the door handle would announce the arrival of her father.

"I hear that you have been a really bad girl today," her father said, as he entered her bedroom. Chrissy remained lying face down on her bed, hugging her pillow and clenching her eyes. "I hear that your mum has already given you a good thrashing," he continued. "She thinks that I should spank you too," he added as he sat down on the bed.

"Let me have a look here," he said, lifting Chrissy's skirt above her waist. "I can see that your mother did a pretty good job here. Yes, that looks sore. It's all right, I am not going to add to it." Then he pulled her underpants down around her legs. "Let me rub that better for you."

Chrissy shut her eyes, as tightly closed as they would go. If I concentrate really, really hard, I won't have to be here anymore. But it wasn't working for her, she was still trapped there in her body.

27

It was heading into September, and the "I want you to meet my parents" conversation had come up again. "I am sure they will like you," Christine reassured me as well as herself. I hoped so because I thought a lot of our problems would disappear.

And so it was arranged, with more than two weeks' notice. We would both take the Friday off so that we could arrive at a reasonable time of day. We caught the train to the nearest city, then the bus to a nearby town, and finally a taxi up to the side of the big house.

Christine was right; I was instantly impressed by the place. If it wasn't for the modern taxi, I might have thought that I'd stepped back in time. Christine led me back past a row of garages. "That is my parent's garage, and above it, that is their flat. This is where I grew up." She told me, "and through there are the stables, I will show you all that later."

"Come on; let's get this over with. Let's go and meet my parents," she added. Christine led me through a door in a wall into an enclosed garden. We passed an eight-foot-high wire cage of quail on our way to the door. She rang the doorbell and opened the door, we stepped into a small entrance way. There were coat hooks on the wall and a few shoes on the floor.

"Come on up when you are ready," Mrs Wilson's voice called out. We discarded our coats and shoes and climbed the flight of stairs to the 'lion's den'. Both of us hoped that this might go well, yet both of us were somewhat apprehensive.

"The kettle is on," Mrs Wilson announced as I was introduced to her. We were led into the living area where Mr Wilson awaited our arrival in one of the easy chairs. We had tea and a single biscuit each and twenty questions. They quite rightly wanted to know who I was and what strange spell I had woven over their daughter.

The flat was furnished with antique cabinetry, passed down from a previous generation. There had been a cabinet maker in the family. A very nice working grandfather clock, a more contemporary settee, and two matching armchairs.

I explain how, unfortunately, my father had died when I was twelve, and how we had come to be in England. I said, "I am sorry to say that my stepfather's advice was, 'don't waste your time with education, go out and get a real job.'" I was sorry too that his assurance that my naval training would be in high demand when I returned to civilian life failed to be correct.

"I'm sorry to say" was a figure of speech, but in their eyes I was always apologising for myself. In fact, I was simply giving them a brief history of my life and trying not to make anyone too big a villain in the telling of my story.

Of course, they were very pleasant about the whole encounter, at least to my face. Christine's father had little to say to me while her mother explained the plans for the rest of the weekend. It was going to be a long weekend under the magnifying glass. All I could do was to submit to the examination. Though I was beginning to get the picture that the deck was stacked against me and that I had been prejudged.

28

Finally, Christine offered me a break. "Come on, let's show Colin around the gardens before dinner," she said. We headed out, first into their private garden patch, then on into the formal gardens of the house itself. They were beautifully laid out around a lake, complete with paths that wandered through the various features of the gardens.

From one vantage point, you looked across the lake to the small church that sat on top of an embankment. Around the next corner, you viewed the back of the house with its majestic terraces leading to the large glass French doors. At no time did you see any other buildings, just carefully manicured gardens, stone walls, and water features.

Mrs Wilson flitted about like a butterfly with a sense of pride, this is my domain, look at how I live. Mr Wilson was more at home out here in the garden; this was his work, and for the most part, he had created the plants and pathway that we were walking along.

Christine surprised me yet again, naming the plants as we passed by. First the English name and then the Latin. I could perhaps tell a rose from a poppy, but that was the extent of my knowledge. So we all got to relax a while before going in for dinner. The initial tension was broken; let the weekend unwind at its will.

Dinner was a simple, Friday night, family dinner. Fresh vegetables from the garden with some meat, and gravy for good measure. After dinner, we watched a little television, nothing that we would have been likely to watch at home. A few more questions during the evening and some general conversation, then it was time for bed.

I lay in my made-up bed on the settee, listening to the ticking of the grandfather clock. Listening to it chime on the hour. Wondering if things were as bad as they seemed to be. Was there something I could think of to brighten my prospects? I finally fell asleep after the twelve o'clock chimes, only to wake early to the sound of the peacocks calling out.

Breakfast was a couple of quail eggs with some toast. That was a special treat for my benefit. Also a mug of instant coffee, as a concession for Christine and I. It was a foggy morning, but after breakfast, Christine said, "Come on, we'll take the dogs for a walk." The dogs were a pair of timid whippets.

I took my camera, and we walked out and around to the west of the house. We climbed the hill until we were looking down at the front of the house, at the stone eagle that sat perched high above the front entrance. It looked somewhat surreal in the fog. I also shot some pictures of Christine and the two dogs, walking off into the distance in front of me. That felt too much like a premonition, and so I posed her at the top of the hill. The two whippets are pulling on their leads and all three looking off into the distance.

29

At lunch, I was asked, "Can you ride?"

"Yes, sure," I replied. The truth of the matter was that I had sat on several horses as they walked along the side of the road or across a field. I had even had a horse run away with me, and I stayed on, clinging to the saddle until it slowed back to a walk. How was I to know what it meant when they asked me, "Can you ride?"

"Great," Mrs Wilson said, "I thought that after lunch, we could take some horses from the stable and explore the estate."

So that was just what we did, all four of us were out through the gate and heading up the hill in front of the house. It was of course, immediately obvious that I couldn't ride. While the three of them sat firmly in their saddles, I bounced around with every little dip in the ground.

"Perhaps we better just stick to a walking pace," Mrs Wilson declared.

I was grateful I wasn't going to be further challenged. A quick canter and I may have been left in a heap on the side of the hill. As it was, the only thing that was bruised was my ego.

The strange dynamics of the weekend continued, with private conversations and sidebars that I was never privy to. I am sure I would have done better if I had never tried to live up to their expectations. Christine's attempts to groom me would never have been enough and had perhaps done more harm than good. But then my age and my previous marital status were enough for them to find fault with, even if everything else was in my favour.

So, Saturday was not the greatest, and Sunday, well, at least we would get to go home on Sunday. But first Christine announced to me, "I thought that we might go hunting in the morning, I used to like that when I was younger. It was my chance to be out and run free across the fields. You don't have to try and keep up," she added. "There will be lots of people walking on behind. My mother doesn't run with the hounds; you can hang back with her."

Mr Wilson belonged to the local hare hunt. A pack of hounds would run across the fields looking for the scent of a hare. Once they picked up the scent, they would give chase with excited howling. At this point, the members of the hunt would join in the chase in the hopes of being present for the kill.

Happily, there was no kill on this occasion, just a couple of exciting moments as the hounds picked up a new scent. For the most part, Christine was far in front of me, happy to run free. But on rare occasions when the scent was lost, and the hounds wandered aimlessly, she would drop back and walk with me. We did a lot of walking together in those days, and as we walked along, we held hands.

Apparently, one does not hold hands on the hunting field. Just one more black mark on my blemished scorecard. How was I to know?

After a light lunch, we were finally on our way. Mr Wilson had consented to drive us to our bus stop. This saved us a taxi fare, but it was no big send off. We still had a long bus ride to the train station and a long train ride home.

Christine sat silently on the bus ride, crestfallen. It was obvious from the Friday night that she wasn't going to get the approval she was seeking. I tried to say something that would make some sense of it all. Something that would ease us into a conversation about what had just happened.

"It is all right, it doesn't matter what they think," was all she would say. But it obviously did matter to her. It was a long, quiet journey home.

30

"Do you still need your parents' permission to lead your life?" I asked. By now I was losing patience with the 'I am leaving you' story.

"It is not just my parents," Christine declared, but she was at a loss as far as giving me any real reason.

Is this the way it ends? I asked myself. The key was on the table, her bag was packed, and she had phoned for a taxi. I was mad and frustrated, and at a loss for anything to say. Her parents were a huge part of her life, and I was just this interloper.

Christine was mad at me, for wanting her so, and she was mad at herself, torn between her heart and her parents telling her that her feelings for me were misguided.

The doorbell rang, it was the taxi. "I've got to go," Christine said with a brief apologetic glance at me. She picked up her bag and headed towards the door. She looked back towards me as if to say 'Do something, make things right,' and then she was gone.

I wandered around aimlessly for about twenty minutes, somehow hoping that I would find some sign of her, some hint that she was not really gone. Then I sat down and cried.

Her parents knew nothing of her history with the previous boyfriend, the one that they had liked so much, and nothing of her history with me. I was just someone that she had met at the hospital.

I hadn't made too much effort to get her back into my life before. Just dropping off that love song on the door handle to her room. She had left, and then things happened, and we were back together. But maybe this was it! If she was going to listen to her parents, how was I to compete with them? I wasn't privy to what they had said to her. I could guess some of it, the age factor, but what else. Could they really be concerned about the fact that I had been married before? Christine never was.

What else could I do? If it was over, it was time that I started to remember who I was as a single man. It was time to learn how to flirt again. It was time to do something new with my photography. I had a life before Christine. Time to do something new: I opened the Yellow Pages and found a riding stable within cycling distance. I booked myself a riding lesson.

How much should I do to try to win her back? Was this all in a losing cause. I should be old enough to know better, but instead, here I am, hurting a little more each time she goes.

31

There was no sign or word from her, and I was at a loss as to what I might do. But I knew that her intake of nurses had arranged a dinner out to celebrate the end of a big block of exams. It was to be held in a restaurant, in a hotel about five minutes' walk from my place.

I bought a single red carnation and kept it in my fridge until I was sure that the dinner was well underway. Then I walked down to the hotel reception desk and asked them if they would kindly deliver it upstairs to her. "No, no note, thank you, she will know what it is all about." Then I turned around and headed home.

It was less than an hour later, my phone rang. "Thanks for the flower," it was Christine's voice on the line. "Do you mind if I come by later when we're finished here?" she asked.

"That would be nice," I told her.

It was as simple as that. Christine arrived, straight from the dinner, and we were living together again. It hadn't solved any problems, like how to deal with her parents. It hadn't even told us if that was the only problem or even the main problem, but I had every reason to believe that it was.

Bit by bit, Christine's things filled the wardrobe and the drawers again, and we got on with our lives together, but without making any progress on the mystery of how to stay together. In fact, we weren't even talking about the long term.

Yes, we talked about how we wanted our lives to unfold. What we would like to be doing in the future, but we hadn't talked about marriage, or being in a permanent relationship with each other. Yet, somehow that was what it felt like we were working on. Why else did we keep getting back together?

But nothing had changed, the sexual problem would reappear from time to time, I would get mad about it. Christine would freeze completely, unable to respond to my questions, unable to move, and that would just make me angrier until I had to storm off. I cooled down just as quickly as I got mad and soon I would be back in bed.

Then Christine would roll over, throw her arm around my waist, and it would all be forgotten until the next time. And back then it seemed there was always the next time. As well as a next time to break up, a next time to get back together. Oh, and that recurring conversation, "I wish you were younger, I wish you were older."

If I had been any younger, I would never have survived the ups and downs, the highs and the lows of life with Christine.

32

It was heading into winter, and although Christine had spent most of the last winter here, I thought if we can survive a winter in this flat we can survive anything. The single pane sash cord windows that never quite fit their frames, the twelve-foot ceilings. The lack of any adequate heating system, or running hot water.

I had one electrical convection heater that I could move from room to room. I might use it in the evening to heat the living room and then, half an hour before bed, take it upstairs to take the chill off of the bedroom. But that didn't work for the bathroom, my big wind tunnel of a room with the cast iron bathtub. So, I bought a paraffin heater to go in there, something to make the room more bearable, especially on bath nights.

The kitchen had a gas stove, and if it ever got really cold, we could shut ourselves in there, with the gas burners lit. Then, of course, there was the old pot-bellied stove in the kitchen, which could heat the room and the water, except it was impossible to keep it running for any length of time. Finally, there was the open fireplace in the living room. It was great for the occasional romantic evening but carrying coals and firewood up from the backyard every day was a time-consuming chore.

Then there were benefits and compensations. Snuggling closer underneath the blankets, and not wanting to get out of bed for anything. On weekends, turning the heater on and rushing downstairs to make the coffee and then rushing back to bed to cuddle until the room warmed up.

Things started to happen towards Christmas. There were plans to make, decorations to think about, a larder to stock. There were office parties and family gatherings, and a friend or two with parties to attend. There was a skittle event for someone's birthday party. Then there was a dance or two, and at every event we were a couple, enjoying the chance to be out together.

The mandarins reappeared, and there were nuts in a bowl. Christmas cake along with a little wine and a few cans of beer, just in case we had a visitor. There was our Christmas tree, sparsely decorated, with a few beautifully wrapped presents appearing underneath it for the two of us. One Christmas stocking hung either side of the fireplace, one for each of us.

This was to be our first Christmas together, really together; Christine had gone home to her parents last year for the four-day break. This year it was all about us, and we were making plans. We let it be known that it was an open house at our place over the holiday, that people were welcome to drop by, anytime. Call in on your way past for five minutes or stay the afternoon or evening.

Christmas Day, Eve and her boyfriend came around. We watched a film together, had Christmas dinner, shared some Christmas cheer and played some cards. No one else made an appearance; the day fell far short of what we had hoped. But it was pleasant for what it was, the four of us made the most of it.

33

Boxing Day, we had left people with the impression that we would be home for the whole of the holidays. No one had shown up on Christmas Day, would it be any different today? My family would be at home, and I was sure that it would have been a better option. What were we going to do with ourselves all day?

We ate breakfast and Christine was unusually distant and quiet. It all seemed a little strange, surreal, an anti-climax. Of course, I just thought that she was as disappointed as I was. I should have taken her to my family's get together. There would have been a Christmas spirit in the air at my mums, for sure. It would have been fun.

Suddenly Eve was there again; this was unexpected. Nothing had been said about her coming by. The sombre mood deepened. The two of them were facing me. Eve was there for moral support. I am leaving you, Christine announced.

She had never called in the troops before. Was it just because this was the most settled Christine had ever been? Almost everything that she owned was there. We had started to accumulate things; there had never been that wrinkle before. Who was going to keep what? Both of our record collections had been mixed together. There was sorting to do.

I sat in the kitchen in shock. I hadn't seen this coming, perhaps I never saw the breakups coming. Perhaps I was too naive; perhaps I was too optimistic. I was aware of the subdued chatter of Eve. I was aware of the growing pile of items by the door. I was consulted once or twice, I was informed that this or that was to go or stay. It wasn't these bits and pieces that were bothering me.

Finally, the two of them stood before me. "I think that I have everything," Christine announces.

"You are just going to go without talking to me about this?" I asked.

"There is not much to say," Christine replied, looking down at the floor.

"Well, I have something I want to say to you," I told her.

Christine looked across to Eve. "Go on down," she said, "I won't be long."

"Are you sure?" Eve asked.

"Yes, I'm sure," Christine told her and Eve disappeared out the door. "It is nothing that you have done," Christine announced, "and it is nothing to do with my parents. It is me; this is what I want to do. This is my decision."

I raised my voice; I expressed my anger. I said things I

should never have said. I said things that I regret ever having said to anyone and Christine stood there and took it. She answered back in a quiet way. She defended her decision, but she was firm. She couldn't express why, but it was what she wanted. This really was it, this time.

"Well, I have had enough of this! You had better be sure because if you come back again, you are going to have to marry me," I told her.

34

There was this vast hole in my life. This emptiness that nothing was going to fill. I wandered around the big empty flat. There was nothing of hers left behind, the bathroom sink, nothing, no toothbrush. The one thing that had given me hope in the past, but it wasn't there.

I lay on my bed and cried, I rattled around the big empty rooms, and I sat in the living room and cried. I was numb, I was lost. I didn't know what to do with myself. There were still more days until the Christmas break was over. I could do with work to distract my mind, but I wasn't fit to be with people. Besides, I worked almost directly across from the nurses' quarters.

This had happened many times before, what made this different? She has come back how many times? Three, four, I'd lost count. I tried to console myself with thoughts that she'll come back, just give her a few weeks. Two, three weeks, she will be back. Something had always happened before to bring us back together.

Though somehow this felt different. She hadn't just come back from a visit to her parents. There wasn't an old boyfriend involved. A new boyfriend, I didn't think so. We were living together; we spent all of our spare time together.

It is what I want, she'd told me. I had to find a way to believe her. How had we been so close, just days ago? How had things seemed so right? Was it just me? I was lost for answers. Suddenly I didn't know what to do with myself, what could I do, what could I have done differently?

Put a positive spin on it, I told myself, perhaps there had been a letter with the Christmas card from her parents. They didn't like our relationship one bit. I was older for goodness sake; I was nearer her mom's age. I had been married before. I was never going to amount to anything. There are lots of young men out there your age. You are never going to find someone while you are living in sin with him.

So, I went to work, and I tried to concentrate on what I was doing. I walked past the nurses' quarters and tried not to take too much notice of them. I walked down the long drive from the hospital every evening with Christine in my head and my heart, but no sign of her.

Then I heard that Fleetwood Mac was playing a concert, up the country, that June. It had only been a few weeks that we had been apart, she will come back I'm sure. And what better a surprise than tickets to a big concert. A band that both of us loved. I managed to get myself the twenty plus miles to the nearest ticket office, the day they went on sale, and I bought two tickets. Tickets to Fleetwood Mac live in concert.

Then I started to learn how to live without her. I poured myself into my photography. I found some models to photograph. I did some work for my friend down the road. Creating shots of the new clothing he was getting in. Photographing girls in leotards, bikinis, one-piece jumpsuits. It helped; it all helped, but it wasn't anything that I wouldn't have done with Christine at home.

35

There was one girl; she was beautiful and blonde and married. She loved to model, and she was easy on the eye. She had an outgoing personality that made her easy to work with. We shot some pictures, and we talked. She started to confide in me. Warmth and friendship was developing between us. She came back to see the results of our shoot. "Let's shoot again," she said.

I orchestrated a couple more photo shoots. Then we started to spend time together without the photography. She invited me to join her in a twenty-four-hour dance marathon for charity. "Me? Not your husband?" I asked.

"I want to do it with you," she responded. She confided her husband was possessive and controlling. "He follows me; he spies on me. I'm becoming scared of him." Perhaps I should have been too.

This wasn't what I wanted, but somehow it helped to fill the void. I had always enjoyed the chase. She needs someone to hold her and tell her that everything will work out. She needed to feel the warmth of unconditional love. I held her, and I flirted with her. I made her smile and tried to let her feel good about herself.

We did the dance marathon together and raised some money between us. Fifty-five minutes of dancing, then a five-minute break to do whatever you needed to do. A trip to the bathroom, a couple of mouthfuls of food, something to drink. Then back on the dance floor, to keep moving through the next fifty-five minutes.

The first eight hours were easy enough, enjoy the music, sway and talk. Everyone was in a good mood. Then about six in the evening, it started to have the feel of a regular night out at a nightclub, there was a party going on. But the bystanders and the supporters started to drift away about midnight. The tiredness started to creep in, and it was tough to keep going, sometimes. Indeed, a few people dropped out, but we kept on. The DJ slowed the music, and we moved to the rhythm in each other's arms.

After that, we continued to see each other when we could. I would walk home from the hospital for lunch, just to spend half an hour with her. We kissed, we petted, and we eased each other's pain, but we stopped short of becoming lovers. We recognised how much more complicated it would have made each other's lives.

I hadn't seen Christine except for one time on my walk from the hospital. It must have been three months into our separation. I had just left the hospital grounds and at the other end of the long road, leading towards town, I saw her. She was walking towards me, on the opposite side of the road. In a green blouse and matching skirt, she was tall and slim and beautiful.

It was painful, watching every movement without appearing to take the slightest notice. I felt too that she was watching me out of the corner of her eye, just as I watched her. But she did nothing to stop me. Call me over, say something, do something, my heart was crying out. Maybe this was it this time.

So, I kept seeing my married lady. Sometimes at lunch and sometimes at the weekend, almost never in the evenings. Though never for more than an hour or two. We grew close but, except for the dance marathon, we never saw each other outside the shelter of my place. Somehow, I felt that I was the crutch that she leant on. But could I ever really mean that much to her if she were free?

36

I was now six months in this vague fog, trying to find my way back to the single man I had been a year or two ago. This should have worked out for Christine and I. Another time, another place. A few years closer in age. Was it just because I was mature enough now for a true relationship? But I had one last card to play: tickets to Fleetwood Mac.

It was worth a try; I had nothing else to lose. I decided

I would take one last trip to the nurses' quarters and ask her if she would like to go with me. No strings attached, just a pleasant evening out at something I knew we would both enjoy. Someone was pounding on a drum, just outside of my ear, or was that my heart, beating so loud in my chest, as I made my way down the corridor to her room.

I knocked, no reply, no noise from the room; this wasn't in the plans. I waited, a little panic hit me, as I was running out of time. Then a fellow nurse of hers turned the corner and looked at me with a question on her face. What do you want? She didn't have to say it; it was written there. "I was looking for Christine," I stated, as casually as I could.

"Oh, she has gone home to her parents, I believe," she stated, moving off.

I was crestfallen and relieved all at the same time. I had left it too late. What could I do? I couldn't phone her parents, they didn't have their own phone. Who didn't have a phone these days? A neighbour, she had once given me their neighbour's phone number, in case of an emergency. I will phone the neighbour, and I will ask to speak to her.

Courage Colin, courage, 'a faint heart never won a lady.' I can't believe that I'm doing this. The phone was ringing in my ear, and my heart was pounding too. Why couldn't they keep time with each other?

"Hello." It was Gladys; I had met her the one and only time I had been there with Christine. Would she remember me?

"Hello, Gladys, this is Colin, I was wondering if you wouldn't mind, I would like to speak with Christine."

"Oh well I know that she is home this weekend, so I'll go in and see if they are there. Would you call back in thirty minutes? That should be plenty of time."

What if she won't come to the phone, what if they have gone out somewhere, what if...? I have done this now; I'm committed. I sat there a nervous wreck, watching the clock tick. Where there is hope, there's… how does that saying go? I dialled the number. She can only say no. It is ringing, one, two, three.

"Hello," it was Christine's voice.

I explained that I had bought these tickets, way back in January, hoping that she might come back and well I had bought them with her in mind. "Would you like to go to see Fleetwood Mac with me?" I asked. I expected a straight 'No.' I had prepared myself as best I could.

"Oh, this is kind of out of the blue," Christine was saying. "Can you give me twenty-four hours to think about it? I will give you my answer tomorrow. If you call me back, this time tomorrow, I will be here to answer the phone."

I called again, twenty-four hours later, twenty-four hours to the minute.

"It was nice of you to ask," Christine said, "but it wouldn't be fair to my new boyfriend. I'm seeing a doctor now and well…" her voice tapered off. "I would love to see the program though, if you wouldn't mind buying one for me. Oh, and if you see me around somewhere, do stop and say hello. I would still like us to be friends."

37

I hung up the phone and sat there. I guess that really is it. Nothing left to do. A lonely tear rolled down from my eye. But this is what I had expected. Indeed, I had expected a straight 'No.' Worse, I wasn't even sure that Christine would have come to the phone. She did come to the phone; she took a day to think about it. I can't imagine that her parents were very happy with me phoning, even so, she took the time to talk with me.

Two tickets to a great concert and no one to take. I asked my married friend, she would love to go, but there was no way she could get away from her husband for more than an hour or two. That's ok, the ticket was for Christine. I will go on my own, and I will have her empty seat beside me. The thought crossed my mind to stand outside the venue and try to sell the ticket, but no, I really didn't want some stranger sitting next to me, in Christine's seat.

It was Fleetwood Mac at their very best, a stunning concert. They played some of their older stuff and something from the new album, but Rumours they played in full. I bought the program to take back with me, on my bittersweet drive home. I didn't even turn the radio on. I drove in silence, not wanting to dilute the sound of the concert still running in my head.

A day or two later, I snuck quietly into the nurses' quarters and hung the plastic bag containing the program over Christine's door handle. I didn't feel up to seeing her, so just in case she was in her room, I was careful to not even let the handle squeak. Then I slipped quietly away, leaving her to discover what she had missed in her own time.

Now what, I asked myself, more of the same. Lunch with my married lady friend, evenings alone in front of the television. My empty bed and equally empty weekends. I am going to have to find my way back to the person I was before. Who was that again? I'm not sure that I remembered.

Then it happened. One day I had walked home at lunchtime to see my married lady friend. Half an hour and I needed to be walking back. Even then and I would be overstaying my allotted time. Luckily work was relaxed about timekeeping, as long as you didn't do it every day. There was a certain amount of work that needed to be completed on any particular day, and you did it. Seldom did it mean staying late, but if you stretched out your lunch hour, that was your concern.

Things were going on at home, and she needed to talk. She had a one-hour lunch break, and we used it all. There were tears, and I tried to reassure her, then she threw her arms around my neck and cried. Somehow something will work out,

I told her as I let her out of the door. Then a minute later I headed back myself. I am pushing my luck this time, I told myself as I hurried through town towards the hospital.

Stepping out of Bath Place Lane, the shortest route back and into a clearing, there she was, Christine. Right in front of me, with no time to think about it. No time to hide or wonder what to do, and no time to assess the situation. There we were face to face on the sidewalk.

"Hi, how are you doing? Thanks for the program. How was the concert?"

"It was great," I replied, "I only wish that you could have been there."

Then with that Christine threw her arms around my neck and cried. "I really miss you," she sobbed. I could feel her tears running down her face to where our cheeks met.

"I miss you too," I offered. I pulled back and looked at her face, her tears were still running, and she looked down and away.

"Can we talk?" she asked. "Can I see you after work tonight?"

"I will come over when I have finished work," I offered. "But now I am already very late, I will see you soon." I rushed off, with a lightness in my step that hadn't been there for a long time.

38

We didn't need to analyse what had happened or why. We both knew that a lot of it had to do with her parents. We had to solve that mystery this time. We could never move forward until we had decided how to handle this issue. But for now, we were back where we belonged in each other's arms.

I was just happy to be living in the moment. Let the pain go, and enjoy being back with Christine. I was not thinking of anything that was said in our last hour together, six months before. But apparently, Christine hadn't forgotten everything I said.

It was our first Friday night back together. Bath night; it was always a special time together. A long soak together in the tub. The bath was run, extra hot water was boiling on the stove, and I was making coffee. Christine had climbed into the tub; I was still dressed as I carried in the coffee. I placed the coffee down within easy reach on the side of the bath.

"I'll be right back," I said.

"Aren't you forgetting something?" Christine asked.

I stopped in my tracks. I was drawing a blank, forgetting something? My mind was rapidly searching.

"Shouldn't you be getting down on one knee?"

I hadn't even thought about it, but that is what I had said. If you come back, this time, we are getting married.

Happily, I had no time to think about it or second guess myself. I dropped to one knee and reached into the bath water. I took her hand and asked, "Will you marry me?"

"Yes," she said, and we both smiled. She glanced down into the water but looked up again, just as I leant across and kissed her.

I was elated! Suddenly it was a lot more than just being back together; we were opening a whole new chapter in our lives. Now the mystery of dealing with Christine's parents became somewhat more pressing. But how? We had known each other for two years now, and we were no closer to a solution.

So, we started to talk as an engaged couple. No longer you and me, now it was us. Perspectives started to change; priorities changed too. Now I could enjoy the here and now, but with one eye on the future. We have a future together. It was what I had always wanted but hadn't dared to dream.

39

I had a female friend, someone I had known for several years, someone with a good head on her shoulders. So, Christine and I invited ourselves around for a chat with her. If Maggie couldn't help us, I was at a loss to know who could.

Maggie of course already knew some of our stories, so we announced our engagement to her. Now how do we cope with this issue? Where do we go from here? We were sitting in this delightful setting of antiques, and except for the clothes we wore, it could have been a hundred years ago. I knew that there were a television and a telephone there somewhere, but you would be hard pressed to see them.

"OK," said Maggie. "Here is what I would recommend that you do. You both sit down individually, and you each write a letter. You tell her parents of your love and your decision to marry. Tell them that you would both really like them to be there, that you would both really like their support. Then you must leave it to fate. Post your letters at the same time, it would be most effective if they arrived together. I think that they will come around."

We took her advice; we wrote our letters. What else could we have done? And then we waited. It took a while, or at least, it seemed to be longer than it was, but Christine got a letter. Of course her parents wanted to be there, and they wanted to be part of our lives. It made a huge difference; Christine breathed a big sigh of relief.

The wedding would likely be a full year away. There was no hurry; we were living together, and not much would change when we did become man and wife. But now we could move forward with more confidence.

However, there was something else that started to weigh on my mind almost right away: money. Money had never been very important to me. I enjoyed my job and found a lot of satisfaction in my work at the hospital. I couldn't ask for a better group of people to work with. But I was earning near to minimum wage. What of the future? We are going to want to create a nice home together; we may very well want to start a family.

I could see a degree of frustration was going to start to build, and it started almost immediately, with the necessity of buying an engagement ring. It had not been that long ago that her previous boyfriend surprised her with an engagement ring. It had looked very lovely, and there was no way I was going to be able to afford to compete with his ring.

We wandered hand in hand through the town centre, window shopping, glancing at the rings in the jewellery stores. There was obviously nothing within our budget, not even close. Then one afternoon we stopped and looked at this tray of second-hand rings. It was a good jewellery store, and honestly, I was surprised that they even had second-hand rings.

"That would be nice if it was all diamond," I said, pointing to one of the rings in the tray.

We were looking at a gold band that circled around to pleasantly shaped shoulders, but then where the diamond solitaire should have been, there was a lump of what looked like silver solder. A tiny chip of a diamond in the centre.

"Let's go in," Christine suggested.

It was cheap, embarrassingly so. No, not even inexpensively so, it was cheap.

"Can I try it on," asked Christine? The sales clerk brought it in from the window display. It had been cleaned up nicely and, if you squinted hard, it didn't look too bad. Christine slid it onto her finger, it fit beautifully, no adjustment need. "I will be proud to wear your ring," Christine offered.

"One day, when we are better off, I will upgrade it for you," I promised.

40

Life was good, and as we settled in together, we were closer than ever. It is true that our sex problem would reappear from time to time even after there was a certain degree of acceptance from her parents of me. Though I still believed they were somehow the cause of this problem, and that the trouble would fade as we moved towards our marriage.

We started to acquire our own furniture. One of my sisters was upgrading her bed and asked us if we would like to have her old one. It was so much better than the two double mattresses we had stacked on the floor at the moment. Somehow we found an old settee and chair, a wooden framed affair with cushions. My parents offered to refinish the upholstery if we redid the woodwork.

Things started to come together. Christine was collecting for her bottom drawer, and although some of the things might have come in handy, we were still living in our beat-up, run-down flat. Christine still had to pay for her room in the nurses' quarters. We could have used that extra cash, but somehow it seemed more important to appease my future in-laws. Yes, we were engaged, but we were not married. Christine's parents were never going to approve of us living together, living in sin. Yes, we could come and visit them, but I would be sleeping on the living room settee.

Then on a visit to my parents, it was announced that my grandmother was giving up driving. Her car was for sale, and as I was family, any reasonable offer would be accepted. I was told, "Offer her a hundred pounds, she doesn't need the money, and she would be glad to see it stay in the family."

So we had a car. It was clean and in good condition except for first gear and reverse. It was my grandmother's habit to start up in first and make it half way to town before she would think to change up to second. How she had managed to wreck reverse gear, I'll never know. But as long as I remembered to hold the gear stick in place while I reversed, it was fine.

This allowed us a whole new freedom, especially it meant that we could drive up and visit Christine's parents without having to stay the night, and visiting Christine's parents was so very different from our first visit. I was welcomed by her mother with a smile, while her father still kept some distance, but her mother would ask my opinion about this and that. She seemed genuinely more accepting of me.

The engagement ring was shown, and no adverse comments were made. However, they were still very much in the driving seat. We had managed a small victory as they had accepted that we were going to get married. But they were still going to have their say. No white wedding, as I had been married before, but we could have a blessing in church after we had a civil ceremony.

We didn't fight this; it didn't matter. We would have our ceremony, and we would be together. It didn't seem important, but it was. We should have put our foot down. It was our day, it was Christine's wedding, and she should have had her white wedding.

41

Then it was Christine's twenty-first birthday. As it only happens once, I wanted to make it special. I wanted to create a memorable day that she could look back on with pleasure. Of course, there was never much extra money around, but Christine deserved something nice. This was to be our first big celebration together.

The pub, just a two-minute walk from our apartment, had a skittle alley. They were happy to let us use it in return for a minimum food order, knowing they would be selling extra drinks all evening. We booked the room, and then I asked my mother if she would make a cake for the occasion. She was always happy to be involved in these things.

So, the invitations went out. All of my family - parents, sisters and their boyfriends or husbands - plus friends of Christine's and mine. Then, of course, Christine's parents. I was so very surprised when they said yes. It was a twenty-five plus mile drive for Christine's parents and would they want to stay over? Where would they stay? They had never even seen our so very basic apartment. They had never met my parents. Was there any point in panicking?

None of this was secret, I had shared the plans with Christine. We did everything we could to make things work out for us. Knowing that we had such a limited income, I did not want to waste money on a birthday present that wouldn't be fully appreciated. So, I involved Christine in that too. She picked out a painting that hung in a local shop, then she also mentioned that she would like a wristwatch, one to wear out when she was dressed up for the evening. I bought her both.

The evening arrived, and so did both sets of parents, so very different from each other. I worried, what would Christine's mother make of my stepfather? My very opinionated stepfather. Oh, how I hoped that the evening would go off smoothly, but there was nothing I could do about it.

Christine's party began well as people mixed and introduced themselves. The booze flowed, and the food was reasonable. We had canned music, something suitable for most age groups and not too loud. The two groups of parents conversed. I can't imagine what they found to talk about, and I was forever worried that my stepfather would say something outrageous, something that would send Christine's parents heading for the door. It didn't happen.

Later, I glanced across and realised that my stepfather must be on his third pint of beer already. Christine's parents were drinking pop. We mingled with everybody there and chatted happily although I always had one eye on the two sets of parents.

My stepfather continued to drink more than he normally would have, and I wondered if he wasn't as nervous as I was about having Christine's parents there for the first time. He must have said something outrageous or opinionated, probably several times over, but Christine's mum just smiled up at him with a big grin on her face. I am sure she had never met anyone like him.

At the end of the evening, as people were saying their goodbyes, my stepfather called one of my sisters over and waving his car keys in the air said, "Here you go, you had better drive us home."

Christine appreciated her evening, the friends and family, the cake my mother had made for her, but most of all, we both appreciated that the evening had gone off without any disasters.

42

Soon it was Christmas, and this time, I was determined that it would be very different. We had our tree and decorations. We had mandarins and nuts as well as chocolates in a bowl. We had Christine's family's traditional Christmas Eve meal, enjoyed with a glass of wine.

But on Christmas day itself, we went to my parent's place in the morning. After all of the guests had arrived we had to sit in a circle around the living room. Mum would reach under the tree, pull out one present, then read the label. From Santa to whichever of the guest it was for, and we all had to sit there patiently and watch while that gift was opened.

Everyone was treated equally: boyfriends, girlfriends, and family members. Everyone received a main present, opening it one at a time, and then various secondary presents. After the first round, things began to speed up, but it still took the bulk of the morning.

Then Mum declared that she should be cooking, and she handed over the present passing duties to one of my sisters, who promptly passed out the rest of the gifts as quickly as she could. Then we had to each make a neat pile of the presents we had received so that when Mum came back, she could see everything.

The turkey never made it to the table before one o'clock, then by the time we had all had seconds and Christmas pudding it was well after two. All of the girls pitched in with the dishes until there wasn't room to move in the kitchen. The rest of us slumped in chairs in the living room, a classic movie on the television, and a couple of kids causing chaos.

There was a brief break in the proceedings, and then Mum was fixing tea. Cold cuts of turkey, cold ham from the day before, and pickles and cheeses, with mince pies, and Christmas cake. More food than you knew what to do with.

After tea and the table was cleared, the cards came out. There was far too many of us for Canasta, but Mum would get out her box of pennies, and almost the whole family would gather around the table to play Chase the Ace, or Bonk, or other easy, fun, family card games.

It could easily be eleven o'clock, and Mum would be asking, "Who is ready for some supper?" Then more plates of leftovers would appear, the kettle would go on, and we would start to wind down for the day.

43

The New Year arrived and heading into spring was one of those pleasant times when we could just cruise along. Enjoying each other's company, despite the difficulties of keeping our place warm, the lack of running hot water, and the cooling drafts through our ill-fitting windows. At least the gap between the wall and the floor allowed some warm air to come up through. It would not do to let the flower shop get too cold overnight.

Christine studied, although looking back perhaps I could see that her heart wasn't in it. We had our television programs, we had our music. We had our Canasta games with my parents. Then we had a settee and easy chair to start working on. A lot of sanding down of the woodwork, followed by a couple of coats of varnish. My parents had taken the cushions to have them recovered. Christine's parents had lent us an old table, one that had spent many years in an outside shed.

Then besides all of this, we had a wedding to plan. Not that we were to have too much say in the proceedings, but there were things to do and things to get ready. We had agreed on the number of guests, with instructions from Christine's parents. That was easy: immediate family and a few close friends. But then we had reluctantly agreed to their two other demands. We were to be married in a registry office, immediately before a ceremony in the little church on the estate. Christine was not to wear white, I had been married before, or was it because we were living in sin, I don't remember which the deciding criteria was.

Perhaps we should have stood up for what we wanted, but we settled for what they were prepared to offer us. A wedding ceremony in the estate's beautiful little church, followed by a reception in the orangery. We met with Vicar Joss, and he would have been more than pleased to marry us. He had no problem with the fact that I had been married before, but to appease Christine's parent, he offered us a lovely confirmation of our vows immediately after our civil ceremony.

The ceremonies were organised, and Christine's parents would arrange the food, along with access to the house, the tables and seating in the orangery. That left us to sort out the invitations, as well as finding a bridesmaid for Christine and a best man for me. Christine was easy, Eve readily agreed to be there for her. But for me, the best man took a little more finding. I wasn't really that close to anybody, but a female friend's husband from work agreed to be my best man.

So, things started to fall into place. Flowers were ordered from the shop below our apartment. Wedding invites went out. Clothing was purchased. A very short honeymoon was settled on. We kept everything as economical as possible. Christine's parents didn't have a lot to spend on the reception, but it was going to be spectacular. A beautiful small church, just big enough for all of our guests, followed by the wedding breakfast in a stately home.

"What about wedding pictures?" Christine asked. "Who can we get to take those?" We could not have afforded to hire someone.

"I will take them," I announced.

"And how is that going to work?" Christine asked. "Isn't it usual for the groom to be in some of the pictures?"

"I have a friend at work, and I think that if I ask him, he will come along. I could take the shots that I am not in, and I could set up the shots that I am in and have him push the shutter. I would set my camera up on a tripod, compose and focus the shot, set the exposure, all he would have to do is push the button. All it would cost us is the price of one more meal, and this would be his wedding gift to us.

"Sounds crazy, but it will work. Then when I have the films processed, I will put together a wedding album for us to keep."

44

It wasn't going to matter how long I worked in the hospital service. The bottom rung and the top rung of the ladder were the same rungs. No promotion, no career development. It was just a low paying job without prospects, and I was becoming frustrated by it, feeling trapped.

However, there was a glimmer of hope for a better future. The government was running a skills upgrade program. If you could pass the entry requirements, they would send you on a one-year course. Not only was the course paid for, but they also paid for your accommodation and gave you enough to live on.

I had already studied electronics in the navy and done quite well, passing with a good grade. But my qualifications were not recognised when I came out. However, I was sure that the experience would give me a head start when it came to studying, but first, I had to qualify. English language, no problem. Basic arithmetic, no problem. But entry to the course required that you understood algebra and calculus. I had never studied either.

My stepfather's advice to me had been, "Go out and get a real job. Don't waste your time with an education." Then it wasn't so much advice as it was a demand. "You'll love the navy." I didn't.

"You'll be in demand when you come out again." I wasn't.

So, having discovered exactly what I needed to learn, I armed myself with course books. I then went cap in hand to the microbiologist at the lab, and as I knew they would, several readily offered to help me learn.

I studied at home, and I checked in with my volunteer tutors for clarification whenever I was stuck or hadn't understood a concept. Little by little, it became easier. The fog cleared, and I was able to work through the problems on my own. I gained confidence, and when I was ready, I sat the entrance exam.

I passed the entrance exam with a good mark, and I was told that I would be accepted into a course when a place became available. The next course would start the following summer, almost a full year away, at any one of the many training facilities dotted around the country. Anywhere will do, I declared, just so long as I can upgrade my skills.

One full school year studying electronics. A City and Guilds certificate to show for my efforts, my own basic toolkit supplied as part of the course and practical experience along the way. I was excited and looking forward to the course, but that was next year. Now I had a wedding to look forward to.

45

It was our wedding day. The sun was shining out of an almost clear blue sky. A beautiful October day, we had been lucky with the weather. Christine had gone to stay with her parents the day before, as it wouldn't do for us to see each other before the wedding. So there I was driving myself up to the registry office, in a town I only vaguely knew, some thirty miles from home.

There was this incredulous moment of realisation - this is really happening. A paradigm shift as if I had passed into a parallel universe, passing from my old reality into this new one. I was travelling hopefully, and I could have stayed in that moment forever.

But then there I was, outside the registry office. Christine looked stunning, in a beautiful burgundy dress, with a bouquet of freesias in her hand. Her mother stood next to her with a 'pleased as punch' expression on her face and her father looking a little lost and out of place standing on the other side.

We walked into the hallway of this grey granite building, right on time, and as we waited, Christine began to shake. The flower petals trembled visibly in her hands. The registrar appeared, and that just increase the now obvious tremors.

"A little worried?" the registrar asked. "That is completely natural," she reassured us both. I was beginning to wonder if the wedding was going to happen after all.

"Let's just step into my office a minute," the registrar suggested. "We can run through the ceremony with you." Which translated into, you can have a moment to collect yourself. She was great, totally reassuring and patient. A calming influence as I sat there and held Christine's shaking hands. At that moment I would not have been surprised to hear Christine say, I can't do this. But she took some deep breaths and calmed herself while the registrar explained the process.

"I am ready now," Christine declared. Then with a quick, furtive glance at me, she stood and hugged me tight and out we went.

Her parents greeted us with concerned looks on their faces, but they were quickly reassured, and we went into the civil ceremony. Brief and succinct, but both of us hugely relieved to have completed our wedding vows. Perhaps it was just as well that we had had this little private ceremony out of sight of the rest of the gathering that would await us at the church.

We signed the paperwork and her parents signed as our witnesses; then and there we were presented with our marriage certificate. Our passport to the next stage of our lives. Out we went, stepping into the fresh air then into my car; husband and wife, we drove away.

"Well, we have done it now," Christine declared. "Perhaps now we can relax and enjoy the rest of our day."

46

The tiny private chapel was the stuff of period films. Just big enough to hold our two sets of family and friends. Decorated with two bouquets of flowers, one either side of the altar, sun shining in through the stain glass windows. I stood in a pool of coloured light in front of the altar, along with the vicar, relaxed in the knowledge that we were already married.

Everyone turned to watch as the door opened, then Christine and her father appeared and started the short walk up the aisle. She looked radiant and beautiful, the nerves were gone, and she had a moment or two to enjoy being the centre of attention. A short, soft burst of canned music filled the air.

We recited our vows, carefully crafted and rehearsed. Words that meant the world to us, but without 'obeying' or any of those words suggesting ownership or servitude. The vicar made it sound beautiful and meaningful. There was a magical atmosphere as we exchanged wedding rings and a collective excitement filled the air as the brief ceremony wrapped up.

Then it was down to business as my co-worker Glen and I set about getting the wedding pictures in this lovely setting at the front door of the church. Christine on her own, Christine with her bridesmaid, Christine and myself, then the two of us with her family and then with mine.

With the pictures taken, it was off down the pathway, through the gate and into the gardens of this beautiful stately home. Along the path and up the terrace, to the back doors of the house. Both doors were open wide for us to pass through, hand in hand. On through the chambers filled with the furniture of a bygone era, Dutch masterpieces hanging on the walls. Then into the orangery, laid out with tables set for our guests and us. Decorated with flowers, a wedding cake in the middle of the head table. Off to one side, another table, a collection of wedding gifts.

We finished off the wedding pictures, just a few group shots to be sure we had a picture of everyone that was there. People gathered and dispersed, chattered aimlessly and then found their places at the tables. Sparkling wine and a rich variety of finger food was enjoyed before a couple more pictures of the two of us cutting our cake. A few short speeches were said, but the formalities were kept to a minimum.

"Isn't it time you two were leaving?" someone was asking.

"Yes, we should have been on our way already," we replied. A ride to the railway station was already arranged, our cases were in the car, and so after dozens of hugs and goodbye waves we were off.

Yes, I have the tickets, I reassured myself. Yes, I have the address of the hotel. But no, we don't have a lot of time. "Thank you all," I called out, and we were away.

47

We kept talking, still distracted by the excitement of the day. Our driver missed the turn, and we weren't paying enough attention to have helped him out. It wasn't enough to slow us down by much, but enough that there were two empty seats, reserved for us, but on their way to London empty!

What a great start, but we were able to smile about it. Nothing was going to ruin our big day now. There was another train within the hour, but without our reserved seating. Then too, the hotel transfer was missed, and we had to grab a taxi and pay for a trip that was otherwise included. But we made it. We settled into our room and then despite the fact that we had been eating all afternoon, we asked about food. "The restaurant is closed, but if you like, we can scrounge you up a plate of curry and some rice."

Not exactly the start we had planned, but there we were together, sitting on our bed, drinking bubbly from plastic glasses and eating cold curry. We were happy and relieved. Even with all of the hitches, it had been a lovely day, but it would take time to really realise that, it had flown by so fast.

This was an extravagance, three days in London, and a honeymoon to set us off on the road of married life. We deserved this and more, but money was tight. Indeed, this was the first time I could remember us actually being away overnight anywhere together. Okay, so there was that dreadful weekend at Christine's parents, but we didn't count that. Here we were, husband and wife, and in London. It was the shoulder season, if there is such a thing for tourism in London, and we had managed to find a weekend getaway deal.

The hotel was clean, pleasant and fresh. Not five star by any means, but luxury when compared to our flat at home. Running hot water in the en suite. Warm and comfortable without any sign of a draft. Double glazed windows and a large warm radiator. These are things I could get used to.

It was central to London, an easy walk to many of the attractions and, of course, close to the underground. You could be anywhere you wanted to be, quickly and easily. If only you could figure out that London tube map.

But here we were on the threshold of a new adventure. Full English breakfast in the restaurant downstairs to start our day off right and a map of central London in our hands. So after a good night's sleep and a filling breakfast we set off to explore on foot.

I must admit I was a little apprehensive about being in the big city. Getting lost, crazy big crowds, aggressive panhandlers. Just being totally out of my depth, but that feeling didn't last very long at all. What I found was more of a close village atmosphere.

48

It was a pleasant, dry, partly sunny autumn day. Ideal for a walk and it wasn't far to Hyde Park. We explored and strolled around, hand in hand or arm in arm. It was peaceful and relaxed. Despite it being a Saturday, the park wasn't busy at all. It was idyllic as we reached the banks of the Serpentine, a happy day for the two of us.

Suddenly a distant explosion ripped through the air, destroying the peace of the day. Bringing us back to an unwelcome reality of the world we live in. A brief flurry of distant sirens, and then the day settled back to its quiet, slow pace. We could enjoy our afternoon at least until the evening news.

The hotel bar was sombre to start that evening as news of the bombing emerged. But a large teddy bear of an Australian man with a shock of ginger hair waxed philosophical for anyone within earshot. Then a few stiff drinks helped to relax the mood in the bar.

Later we were entertained by a young and somewhat inebriated man who couldn't figure out how to get himself through an open glass door. The left side of a pair of doors was locked closed, and the right side was wide open, but in his drunken state, he pushed and pulled at the left-hand door. He glanced pleadingly towards the barman and then as people couldn't help but laugh at his dilemma, he tried again. Finally, he stepped back, saw the error of his ways, then laughing at himself he passed unsteadily through the open right-hand door.

Sunday we rode the tube on our way into the theatre district. It was quiet, and we were confident that we had our trip figured out and that we would arrive in good time for dinner and our tickets to Agatha Christie's 'The Mouse Trap'.

At one station the doors opened and in piled a group of eight punk rockers with tattered clothes and spiky hair. We weren't that much older than they were, but we lived in a whole different world, or so I thought. The train rattled off, and they chatted happily among themselves, all eight gathered around a seat for four people across the aisle from us.

Suddenly at the next corner, the train lurched, and one of the young punks flew across the aisle, almost landing in my lap. Then this young punk rocker quickly gathered her wits and then looking down at us and in her best Oxford accent said, "I am terribly sorry." Funny how the world is never quite what it seems.

49

Far too quickly the weekend was over. It was Monday afternoon, and we were on the train and on our way back home. We chatted about the highlights of our honeymoon. Mostly we sat saying nothing at all, cuddled up and holding hands. Later we talked about our immediate future until it dawned on me.

"Many happy returns of the day," I said. For the first and last time, I had forgotten Christine's birthday. Not even a card to give her, but she had forgotten too. Not until that moment had either of us realised it was her birthday!

"You are forgiven," she said, "but don't you dare let it happen again."

Home again and we settled into the same routine. Back to work, Christine nursing and me at the lab. Making the most of our leisure time and planning how we were going to handle my electronics course next year. Depending on where the course would be held, the thought was that Christine would stay home and carry on working and I would get home to see her when I could. Perhaps on a long weekend she could come and see me.

We hadn't been told where the course would be at this point, only that I would be on the next available course. I wanted to get on with it, find a better job, and start earning a living wage. So I had said that I would be willing to go anywhere, just get me on the next available course.

The pressure from Christine's parents was gone. In fact, Christine's mother seemed to look up to me. What do you think about this, she would ask, and what do you think about that? The days of suddenly finding myself a bachelor again were behind me.

So, it was something of a surprise to me to find that Christine's problem being sexual was still there. True it didn't happen as often, maybe it wasn't quite as intense, but it was there. Some nights she froze. If my belief that it stemmed from her parents was wrong, then what? What was happening to her? Was it to do with me?

She still wouldn't - couldn't - talk about it, and all I could do was to try to temper my response to the episodes. The less of a big deal I made of it, perhaps the easier it would become for her to talk. Or would it just fade over time, all I could do is to wait and see.

50

"Good news," I announced, waving a letter above my head as Christine arrived home from work. "Well sort of good news anyway," I corrected myself.

"I have good news too, I think it will be good news, but yours first."

"I am on the next electronics course, starting this summer. Only the thing is, it is in Scotland." Christine paused, there was no immediate response. "I know that it is further away than we had hoped, but at least I am in that course."

"That is great news. We'll figure it out, I don't know, but we will cope somehow."

"I know we will," I reassured her. "Now what is your good news?"

"Well," Christine started, pausing for effect. "I got talking to one of the girls at work, on our lunch break today, and she and her husband are buying a house."

"Yes." Where is this going I thought to myself?

"The thing is, they will be moving out of their rented flat, and she thinks that she could put in a good word for us with their landlord."

"Interesting, tell me more; where is this place?"

"Oh, it sounds lovely, and it is just down the road from here.

It wouldn't be any further to walk to the hospital. It is clean and modern, and it has running hot water, it has windows that fit, and it has a storage heater too. Can we see it, can we?" an excited Christine asked.

"It sounds great, how much is it, did she say?"

"Yes," Christine replied. "But now that I don't have to pay to keep my room in the nurses' quarters, it is not that much more."

"So, when can we see it?" I asked.

"I have told her to please go ahead and ask for us. It is so hard to find somewhere decent to rent. Oh, I do so hope that this will happen for us."

Our luck did seem to have been improving by leaps and bounds lately. We were married and an accepted part of both of our families. We had acquired some better furnishing, even if it was second hand. Even if we did have to put in a lot of work refinishing it. We had my grandmother's car at a very reasonable price. Now it seemed that we might have a much nicer flat to live in, and I was accepted into an electronics course. Life was good.

51

With a lot of help from family and friends, we moved. It wasn't even a quarter of a mile away, but there was a whole world of difference between the two places. As a latter-day hippie and a bachelor, I was content with my job and content with my crash pad. Now I was a family man, and I wanted better things for us. I wanted to be able to afford to have children. I wanted to do all of the things that families do.

There was no longer any place in our new flat that I could easily use as a darkroom. However, it was a three bedroom flat. One bedroom on the main floor and two more upstairs. The larger one of these became my studio. A couple of rickety old light stands with umbrellas and battery powered flashguns. The smaller of the two was our guest bedroom. We had progressed from two double mattresses on the floor when we first met, to two double beds.

We both became house proud, glad to have people around to see our new place. We relaxed into our new lifestyle. We still soaked together in the bathtub, usually on Friday evenings, but now there was hot running water. Sometimes a glass of wine but more likely a mug of coffee and we would lay back and talk. Relax, turn the tap on to warm the bath water, and of course, I would wash Christine's back.

Christine seemed to find a new level of comfort within herself. A new level of confidence and somehow, she felt safe. Safe in her new environment and safety in the fact that she was now a married woman. Her parents had accepted our togetherness. Now she wasn't likely to find herself alone in a room in the nurses' home or trying to make her way in the world without support.

Life was better for both of us, and I was confident that I knew where we were and where we were going. But life was not to be quite that simple.

One night, having gone to bed, as usual, curled up like two spoons in a drawer, I was drifting off when Christine suddenly sat bolt upright.

"What is it," I asked. I thought perhaps she had heard a noise. But in the half-light of our darkened bedroom, I could see she was in a state. Tension gripped her body, then, at last, she glanced across at me, and I knew that there were tears in her eyes.

"I think that I am gay," she said. Then very quickly afterwards, "Are you going to throw me out?"

"No, I love you, I would never throw you out," I replied. I turned to Christine and put my arm around her as she fell into my arms, sobbing. The tears flowed, and she shook with pain and fear and confusion. For a long time, I just held her, then as the tears subsided, I tried to reassure her.

"It will be all right, we will work things out." I had no idea what this would mean for us in the long run. I had no idea what this would mean period! Would I lose her one day to another woman? Was this the source of her sexual problems? My head was in a spin, and I was way out of my depth, but I knew I could be there and support her, for now at least.

52

Now I began to see the bigger picture. So, I had been wrong, all of this time, while I had thought that her parents trying to drive a wedge between us had affected her sex drive. In reality, it had taken all of this time until she felt safe. Finally, she was comfortable enough in her own skin to admit to herself that she might be gay.

It had taken me forever, and finally, I had found the relationship I had always wanted and now? So, this was why Christine was always so comfortable with me photographing young ladies. Also why she showed such an interest in my pictures.

We were so close and so good together. I had done whatever I could to support her, as she had for me. Was I now to be the close friend of two gay girls? Well, so be it! I will be winging it, I will be lost and confused, but I will do what I can to help her.

Christine quickly felt comfortable again, knowing that I was there for her. Knowing that she still had my support. That I wasn't about to throw her out, break up with her, or worse, run around saying, "Oh my god, she is gay."

We talked, and she opened up to me in a new way. Neither of us had any real idea what this was that we were talking about. What could this mean? How this would unfold, or how to deal with this? But in a way, it became easier for me, understanding the underlying cause of our one big problem.

So while everything had changed, nothing had changed for us. We were the same people, with the same routines. Maybe not quite the same hopes and fears, but we carried on much as before. We shared our chores, we watched TV cuddled up together, and we slept like two spoons locked together through the night.

We had our long soaks in the bathtub together. Talking, relaxing, just enjoying being together and it was in one of these soaks, only a week or so later, Christine sat in front of me in the tub. We had our coffee in our hands, both sat up drinking from our mugs.

Without turning her head at all, Christine said, "I think my dad molested me." There was a brief pause. "No, I know my dad molested me." Then she glanced back at me, a tear rolling down her cheek. We both put our coffee down, and she fell back against me. I wrapped my arms around her arms, and pulled her closer towards me, holding her there in protective silence.

What could I say? I was lost twice over. If I had little knowledge of what her being gay really meant, I had none at all about this. I had no idea that such a thing even existed and now what? But somehow, I knew that I was in a privileged position. I was privy to the deepest darkest corners of Christine's life. I had won her trust and allowed her the support to look her own world in the face.

If Christine truly were to turn out to be gay, one day I would have to step aside and let her go. It would hurt, and I would be at a loss as to how to move on, but I could understand and be happy for her even. Now this, what would it mean for us? What would this mean for her?

53

It was a bright sunny day. It was the weekend, and we had the two days off together. We headed out with no special plans to do anything other than a bit of window shopping. Perhaps coffee at a favourite cafe.

We were walking hand in hand as always. Suddenly I felt a gentle tug on my hand, followed by a squeeze. I looked across to Christine. She caught my eye and with a sly grin she nodded in the direction of an attractive girl across the street.

"Um, nice," I declared, then leaning in towards Christine, I said, "You have great taste."

"Wouldn't you love to get her in front of your camera?" Christine asked.

"That would be fun," I offered. "Do you think that she would make a good model?"

"She is lovely."

Then with a timid smile, Christine glanced down, tightened her grip on my hand, and we moved on down the street. The very thing that I feared would pull us apart had started to bring us closer together. I had never perfected the art of surreptitious girl watching while with another woman. Now I didn't even have to try!

It gradually became a subject of open conversation. We talked about women. We talked about our taste in women. Of legs and bums, of soft curves and femininity. We talked about the joy of just spending time with one of these delightful creatures. The feeling of being lost in a smile.

Although they meant so much more to each of us than just being sex objects, we talked about that too. We talked about them in bed; we talked about being in bed with them! Christine was curious and wanted to know what it felt like to hold a woman, naked in your arms. I really did not have the words to tell her.

How do you describe the colour green to a blind man? How do you explain the tang of marmalade in your mouth to someone that has never tasted it? Can anyone else ever understand how your world shrinks around you at the smell of her hair, at the touch of her skin?

But we made love, exploring what this would mean to each of us. Suddenly there was a glimpse of the passion and freedom that we had enjoyed when we first met. A hint of the abandonment that was ours before our relationship had become a serious endeavour.

It was uncharted territory for both of us. But we felt free to explore, having developed a trust and an openness with each other. A whole new world was opening up to us both.

54

"We used to go out for cycle rides as a family," Christine was explaining one night in the bathtub. "We would take some water, and a little snack Mum would pack up, and we would cycle through the country lanes. We might stop at this little waterfall sometimes, or park our bikes and walk through this little woodland. It seemed such a vast adventure to me as a child.

"One Saturday morning, my father had declared, let's go for a bike ride." Christine continued. "'I will go down and get the bikes ready,' he announced.

"It was a nice day in early spring. We didn't often get to go out very far, but I had enjoyed some of these trips.

"'I will go and make some sandwiches,' my mother offered. 'We can make a picnic of it.'

"Then my father came back in and told my mother, 'Your bike has a flat tire, and I don't have a puncture kit to fix it. I will get one on our next trip to town. But it would be a shame to miss this sunshine, so I will take Chrissy out for a ride.'

"There was an instant tension that I just didn't understand. I was too young to make any sense of any of this. Still, my father took me downstairs, and we hopped on our bikes and cycled off.

"Well, we had hardly gotten out of sight of the house when my father called out 'Stop there a moment.'

"He came up beside me, and he told me he was worried that my dress might get caught in the wheel. So he gathered up the front of my dress, and he tucked it down inside my panties." Christine paused and sat there in silence for a moment.

"Then he did the same thing with the back of the dress. I didn't know what it was or why. It didn't feel right, but I simply froze. He had a little grope, inside my drawers, and then we rode off.

"The sides of my dress were not tucked in. They were still flapping about in the breeze."

Christine fell back against me and sobbed. Her body shook, and I knew tears were rolling down her face, although she didn't turn her head for me to see them. Then she sat there in front of me with her head pressed against mine, until she had calmed herself down.

I so wanted to tell her that it was all right, but it wasn't all right, and nothing I could say would make it so. Nothing I could say or do was going to make this memory any less painful. But the one thing I could do was to make her feel safe now, to let these memories be acknowledged.

"He stopped me again and slid his hand into my panties, just to make sure my dress wasn't coming out, he said. Then just as we were arriving back home; he pulled my dress back out. 'We are nearly there, it should be safe now.'

"My mother was furious with me when we got in. I had no idea why. I couldn't understand what I had done wrong."

55

As plans go, this one may not have been very well thought out. I was excited about my course. I was looking forward to it, and I was looking forward to being able to earn a decent living. The sooner, the better, and that is why I had agreed to take the next possible course available, wherever it was.

Christine was to keep on working at her nursing and to stay looking after our flat. We always knew that I would have to go away somewhere for the course, but the thought was that I would stay away all week, do the course and study in the evenings as necessary, then Friday evening after school I would drive home for the weekend. Only to be up early Monday morning and drive back to class.

But Scotland, this was about as far away from home as I could have been sent. If I set out first thing Saturday morning, drove most of the day, I could be home for one evening before setting off back by lunchtime the next day.

I needed this course. I had accepted it; I had handed in my notice at the lab. I was out of work and without prospects, unless I did well in class, passed my exams; then we had a chance at a better life.

"We will work something out," I promised Christine. I had no idea what or how. Can we survive on phone calls and perhaps seeing each other once a month? If we were lucky maybe. Holiday weekends, midterm school breaks?

I held Christine, and there was a tension in her body, but she was being strong.

"Drive carefully, and call me when you get there," she said. "Drive safely."

I climbed into the driver's seat and set off, trying to think only of the long-term benefits. It was a very long drive on my own, and it wasn't easy. A break for lunch, to stretch my legs.

A snack in the car, some music on the radio. But it was easier for me at this point than it was for Christine. It was my new adventure.

Finally, I arrived at a pub, a few miles north of where the course was to be held. Sight unseen, I had booked a bedsitter room with a small kitchenette. There were a small table and two chairs, a couch that pulled out to become a bed and colour television. Everything there had seen better days, but it was clean and adequate.

Downstairs, a pleasant enough public house. A bar on one side with a pool table and dart boards, the other side was the lounge. Most importantly, I had been greeted by a welcoming landlord, and there between the two sides, a coin-operated public call box. I got some change and phoned home to tell Christine that I had arrived safely. There were tears.

56

The course started on a Monday morning. There were twelve of us, males from different backgrounds and histories as well as various different parts of the country. We were given a roll of basic tools, which were ours to keep at the end of the course. We were given our study books and told how the course would be laid out. A mix of theory and practical work, and there would be some help finding work afterwards.

We met our instructor and heard about his background. He seemed pleasant, but most of all he seemed interested in what he was doing. So from everything he told us, I was sure he had the knowledge and the skills to pass his trade on to us.

In the afternoon, we had someone come in to tell us what we would be paid while we were on this course; the when and how of being paid and who to contact if we have a question about anything at all. Questions were asked and answered. It turns out that one of the guys on the course had brought his wife up with him. She was unemployed, and he was getting an extra allowance for her.

"If my wife comes up to join me here, what do I need to do?"

"Just let us know when she gets here," he said rather matter a fact. "You will get an extra," and he threw some figure out in the air for me.

I was scribbling down numbers on my notepad. It will be tight, but mainly because we would have an extra layer of rent to pay: a bedsitter room here and we definitely wanted to have our home to go back to. But subtract one of those rents, and with me on the course and Christine unemployed, we would be as well off as we were when we were both working full time for the hospital.

I would phone home soon and see what Christine had to say, I decided. It was going to be a very long year for the both of us, stuck so many miles apart, and if that was an option, I would really rather have her here. Not much to cook with, not much of anything at all really, but I was sure she could make due.

Such a strange feeling, standing in a call box so far from home and visualising that phone on the sideboard ringing.

"Hello," Christine's voice on the other end.

"Hi, it's me. How are you doing?"

"I can't do this, I can't." I could hear the tears and the stress in Christine's voice. "I want to be up there with you."

"Just tell me what time your train is getting in, I'll pick you up from the station," I said, more than a little pleased with the idea of having her here with me.

"Really, can we do that?" Christine asked.

So I told her what I had found out about the extra allowance I could receive for her, and the wheels of plan B were set in motion.

57

I was waiting for the day that Christine was due to arrive, a week or so to go yet. I had nothing I needed to study, and there was nothing on the television. So I went down to the pub, looking for a pint and perhaps a game of pool.

I shot a couple of games with a local, and I sat there trying to stretch my pint out until closing time which wasn't so far away. Closing time was pretty much the same everywhere. I sat there remembering a couple of weeks back when Christine and I had gone out for the evening, not sure when we would have the chance again.

Usually when the landlord rang the bell for last orders, six people from different tables jumped up and headed for the bar. This evening I fully expected the same. But I was in for a surprise.

Mike was a big cheerful landlord, not likely to have much trouble from any of his customers. He finished serving one couple and then stepping across to the back wall, he hollered out, "Last orders please." He rang his bell, and then he stepped back to the sink and carried on washing glasses. Nobody moved. It was so strange not to see that last minute rush.

I sat waiting still surprised that no one had approached the bar. I was even more surprised when precisely at the closing time, Mike walked out from behind the bar, checked that both of the front window blinds were closed and then locked the front door. Still, nobody moved, I was intrigued. Even more so, when a few minutes later first one customer and then another approached the bar and bought a couple of drinks.

This was obviously normal, at least around here. A group got up from their table, yelled, "Good night, Mike" and walked out the back door. All that closing time meant was that you couldn't use the front door. A car pulled up at the front, someone got out and tried the front door, a quick rattle of the door handle, and then they were back in the car, and the car drove off.

I wasn't entirely sure about this until sometime later. The back door opened and in walked two policemen. They sat in the corner of the bar and ordered a pint each. So this was Scotland. I was living above a pub with strict timekeeping and flexible hours.

Then Christine arrived. We were both so thankful not to have to do this year on our own, miles apart. We would go down to the bar, enjoy a drink, and shoot some pool. We played against each other or were challenged by some of the locals. At weekends there was the added bonus of a singer playing his guitar and introducing us to many a Scottish tune,

Soon Mike offered Christine a part time job behind the bar, helping out at busy periods. It gave her something productive to do and a little extra cash in her pocket. She was allowed twenty hours part time before we would lose any of her allowances. It gave us a reason to be down there without spending too much extra money. At eight o'clock in the evening, Christine could understand every word of every customer. Two hours later it was a different story. After they had a few beers, and a wee dram or two of Scotch in their system, Christine would have to ask Mike for a translation for some of the broader speaking clients.

"I never wanted to be a nurse," Christine announced one evening after we had come back from the bar.

"You didn't?" I asked. She hadn't told me this before.

"No," Christine continued. "it was the only way that I could find to leave home. I couldn't wait to get out of there, and if I could have started at sixteen, I would have. I put my application in just as soon as possible and at a couple of hospitals that were far enough away from home that I couldn't be expected to go home on weekends."

"So we might not have met," I told her.

"No, but this was the first hospital to accept me on a course that started straight away," she added. "There was no work anywhere around our home. I started working at the Golf Club Restaurant when I was sixteen, just to get out of the house. Just to get away."

Christine was hanging her head and closing in on herself as she was telling me this, then she added, "That is where I learnt silver service," and she brightened for a moment with a sense of pride in her achievement, before closing in on herself again.

"The next year I got myself a summer job at a hotel on the north coast. Anything to get away from home. I couldn't start nursing yet," Christine reminded me. "It was so busy in the summer and the days seemed to fly by. I had a few hours off every afternoon, and I would take myself on long walks along the cliff paths."

"Then things started to slow down, my contract would be up soon." Christine paused a while before continuing. "Things were slowing down, the restaurant was closing earlier, and I had more time on my hands. I sat alone in my room; I tried to read. There was no town as such, just this little village. Then I found they would let me sit in the bar, as long as I had a drink in front of me. I was seventeen, and they knew that, but they had no problem serving me cider."

"I made it last as long as I could," Christine looked across at me briefly. "I didn't want to be spending my money, I had saved hard and wanted to take home as much as I could. Then one night one of the guys there came and sat down next to me. He offered to buy me a drink, and I let him. He seemed pleasant, we chatted, and then when I was ready to head up, he said that he would walk me to my room.

"I didn't think anything of it, as I knew that he was staff and staying there too. But then when we got to my door, and we were just saying goodnight, he pushed his way in as I opened my door." Tears were running down her face. "I have never told anyone this before, he raped me." Then Christine fell against my chest and sobbed. I held her tightly until I felt the tension flow from her body.

58

The year continued much the same for me. I understood the course material and found the practical side relatively easy. I felt that I was achieving something, making progress, and was sure that I would find a better job at the end of it.

Christine, on the other hand, had little to do with herself. She didn't know anyone there, and although the people were friendly, she was at a loss to fill her time. A little grocery shopping, a little cooking, the room was so small that it took very little of her time to tidy up.

So she found a local gym with an inexpensive drop-in fee, and she spent some of her time working out. She was slim and fit anyway, an attractive woman in her twenties. She started to mention a girl that she had met at the gym and that they were working out together.

"That's great," I assured her, and I started to probe with some gentle questions. "What does she look like? How old is she?" Just general curiosity. Then the obvious question. "Is she gay?"

"No, she is not gay," Christine said she was sure, that she was not gay.

But that didn't stop her from fantasising about what she might do with her if she were. We started to talk about her when we went to bed. Share erotic fantasies. Christine's interest in sex peaked. It was reminiscent of our early days together.

I enjoyed this time together. What red-blooded man wouldn't? The thought of her with another woman aroused me. Hearing tales, perhaps playing the voyeur, even the idea of a threesome. I had had one very minor encounter with two young girls, long before I had ever lost my virginity.

They continued to work out together, meet up some days for coffee, or just get together for a chat. I heard bits and pieces of conversations from time to time. These explained why this girl was available during the day, what her future plans were, but nothing that told me there was a relationship building.

Then one day towards the end of the course, Christine announced. "I have realised that I am not gay after all." With that, Christine's interest in sex fell away.

59

Finally, the course was over. I had passed with really good marks, despite my lack of studying. For the first time in my thirty-five years, I had a piece of paper that told the world I have a qualification: a City and Guilds in electronics.

We packed the car. The trunk and back seats were full to the ceiling. Then we headed south. I had no idea what was next, but I was hopeful. Both of us were unemployed, but Christine had always been very employable and had always managed to find work. And now I had a piece of paper!

Less than an hour into our journey, a burst of steam came up from under the hood of the car. The temperature gauge shot over to maximum, and I pulled over to the side of the road. This was not the start that I was looking for. Luckily, I was still a member of the AA, and we had the right guy arrive.

"Oh, I can fix that for you, but you will have to come with me and buy a new water pump. What would you like to do?" he asked, but I had little to no choice. I would be spending our rent money as it was. But we had no money for hotels or for garage repairs. This was a lucky break.

So ninety minutes later we were on our way again, knowing

we needed a bit more luck on our side, and if we hadn't realised already, we knew for sure we would have to be very careful with the money we had left.

Back home in our flat and the very first thing we both had to do was to go job hunting. I especially needed to find work that was relevant to my new qualifications. So first thing Monday morning we were off to the job centre. There was hope. They sent Christine off for a job interview straight away. I had to wait a little longer.

But I landed a job, just the thing I needed. It came with a car, an almost new Ford Escort, shiny bright red and no company logo on the side. Not that a logo would have put me off.

The pay was good, added to which was a lunch allowance, and a more-than-generous gas mileage allowance. Enough that I would end up with some extra cash in my pocket each month. There was a lot of territory involved, the whole of the South West of England.

We were servicing equipment that had been sold by or leased from the company. Most of it was newish, and the faults were relatively simple. I had to phone in first thing in the morning and get my workload for the day. But if there were nothing booked, I would have to call back at noon. The morning was mine.

Sometimes I would have unplanned days off. Sometimes I would finish late and have a long drive home, even arriving some two hours late for dinner.

60

"It strikes me that it is a little odd that you can afford a new car, but you can't manage to pay me my rent money," my landlord called out as I was heading for the said car and my day's work.

"Oh hi, I am sorry that it's late. I will catch up very soon now," I promised. "It is not my car, it comes with my new job," I added quickly.

"Please see that you do, I would like my money," he said, giving me a stern stare. "On time preferably."

"I will," I offered. "I have just finished a course, but now that I am back at work, I will be catching up very soon."

And with that, I climbed into my car and set off down the road.

I wondered what they want, I thought to myself. My usual morning call for my workload had been met with a request for me to come up to head office. What was this, week three? I was not aware of any complaints. Everything seemed to be working out fine. It is just routine I am sure.

"Come on in, sit down," my boss greeted me, as cheerful as ever.

"I have some bad news for you I am afraid," he said as I sat in the chair opposite him.

"Oh, have I done something wrong?" I asked.

"No, not at all. I have been very pleased with you."

"However," he continued, "the company has just taken a really bad hit on the stock market, and so there have to be some cutbacks. Last in, first out, as I am sure you would realise."

"Yes, I can appreciate that would be the case," I said.

"You will be getting a bonus cheque, instead of notice, and of course you will be getting paid for the time you have put in."

"Thank you for that," I said as I started to get my head around what was happening.

"So I have to take the car back, straight away," he continued. "If there is nothing else, I will have someone drive you home."

Arriving home, my first task was to drop by Christine's workplace and tell her my bad news. Then it was straight over to the job centre, and back to job hunting. It was not always easy to stay optimistic.

61

The strange thing I have found with bad luck, it so often isn't bad luck at all, but rather a lucky break. A very serendipitous bit of good timing. I had been paid enough for my time worked to catch up with my overdue rent and still have a little left in my pocket. Now I was looking at an advert, 'electronic technicians wanted'.

It was a vague ad; there was very little description of what they were expecting you to do, how much experience you were expected to have. Where exactly was this job? It didn't give much away, just lots of incentive by stating that the money was good.

I needed to get in on the ground floor, I needed to gain some work experience. Honestly, I needed a job, and so I applied and very quickly got a job interview. Then my first surprise; this wasn't a company looking for employees, rather it was a company that supplied qualified technical staff on a contract basis.

Yes, the money was good, but job security, not so much. Still, perhaps I could gain some real experience. Yes, they had a job that they wanted to send me to. No, I didn't get paid holidays, and no, I didn't get paid for sick days. But I would get paid way more than I had ever earned before!

"When are you available for job interviews?" he asked me.

"Any time at all," I replied. "Any time at all."

"Great, expect to hear from me soon," he told me. "I will arrange an interview, ASAP."

So, I thanked him for his time and headed home, not in my shiny red car, but in my own slightly beat up, grey, seen-better-days car. Yet I was hopeful. However, it was still something of a surprise, when walking through the door at home, Christine announced, "There is a message on the answering machine for you."

"You have a job interview, tomorrow morning at ten," the

message on the machine was telling me. Then the voice gave me the name and address of the company. One I had never heard of, in a small village some twenty-five miles away. I got the maps out and made sure I knew exactly where I had to go.

"Ten o'clock," I said to myself, plenty of time to get there. "No rush hour traffic, good."

"I have no idea what this company does," I told Christine. Then I explained what I had found out so far. How I would be working as a contractor, and just how quickly this interview had come about.

"Well, they must be keen to see you," Christine said. Then she walked off to leave me with my head in a spin.

62

I had no idea what to expect. I arrived in good time to find a village that was mainly filled with tourist attractions, and off in one corner the company I had come to see. It looked like an office building, with parking to one side. The sign over the front door gave the name and the company logo, but nothing else.

I stepped through the door and up to the receptionist. As I introduced myself, I noticed much more security features than I was expecting. Do I look smart enough? I asked myself. Will my lack of experience be a problem? I so hoped that this interview would go well.

Suddenly I was whisked through the door and on a guided tour. I was standing in front of a tape deck. But it is like no tape deck I had ever seen before. Six-foot-six tall and two-foot-six wide, with ten-inch reels and one-inch recording heads! All around me were technicians at test benches, with oscilloscopes and machines I didn't recognise.

"One hundred and fifty-four megabits per second," my perspective boss was telling me with pride.

"Wow," was all I could say, as all I knew anything about were little cassette recorders.

"If there are dropouts on the tape, it is smart enough to replace the missing data," he continued. "If the tape breaks or for any reason it stops recording, it will hand the job over to another machine, sitting there on standby."

I am so out of my depth, I was thinking to myself.

"We have a large order to supply NASA, and that is why we are taking on extra staff at the moment. Now let me show you what we want you to be doing," and he waved his hand in the direction of double doors in the corner of the room.

We stepped into a room where six young women sat, each at her own bench assembling tape heads. Parts neatly stacked in plastic boxes. Wires hanging from a rod suspended at the end of their bench, and a hot soldering iron within easy arm's reach.

"This is John, he is doing your job right now, inspecting and testing these tape heads, but he will train you to take over from him." He looked across at me with confidence in me that I wish I were feeling myself. "We'll expect you to be able to take over from him within a week, but he won't be far away if you need any help."

John stood up and shook my hand. "I'll see you soon," he said.

"So, there we are, any questions?" my new boss asked. "Oh, and we supply all of your tools and the white coats I am sure you have noticed, everyone is wearing one."

63

Work went well, and I enjoyed it. It wasn't long before they offered me a permanent position, and I took it. Less money, but more security, I thought. Paid holidays and paid sick days if I need them, not that I was ill very often in those days.

Then driving home one day I was looking at this sign "Affordable starter homes", considerably closer to work than I lived now.

We investigated. Yes, we could get a no deposit mortgage, subject to a house inspection. So at the weekend, Christine and I went to take a closer look.

The houses were small, a one bedroom in a new development at the top of the hill. Some were already sold; a few people had started to move in. But there was a mid-terrace, yet to be finished. A small private backyard. Neighbours either side, but nobody behind us, because we were at the top of the hill, so we could look out over the valley.

We were moving forward in leaps and bounds. Homeowners. Okay, so the place was too small to start a family in, but it was a start. It was much closer to work for us. We both had pretty good jobs, and what's more, they were both Monday through Friday jobs. We had our weekends together.

The one thing we had both always loved to do was dance. Disco, freestyle, smooching on the floor to slow music. There was nowhere close, but it didn't matter. We would drive miles on a Saturday night. There were three different nightclubs in three very different directions. So we would pick one, and we would dance until closing time.

Then we might stand outside one of our favourite clubs and eat bacon and egg butties from this wagon that would sit outside, waiting for the few hungry stragglers. We would drive home hot and tired at two in the morning, and if we had been really hot, we would have a soak in the bath before we crashed for the night. It didn't matter; Sunday morning we could lie in as long as we wanted to.

Oh, and you should have seen Christine. My heart would swell as I walked her out onto the dance floor. She was tall and slim, with the figure of a model. She had a perfect sense of rhythm as she moved to the songs of the time. Songs we both knew so well. I can still see this beautiful, peach coloured satin dress that flowed with her body.

64

"I use to hate Sundays," Christine said one lovely sunny Sunday morning.

We had taken our two folding chairs out onto our back patio with our morning coffee, after a night out dancing.

"Why, because they made you go to church?" I asked.

"No," Christine answered, and then fell silent for a while.

"No, going to church was bad enough," she continued. "Sitting through the sermon was okay. But afterwards, when people gathered outside the church, 'Oh, what a lovely family', they would say.

"I would want to scream out, sometimes.

"Instead, I would stand there staring down at my shoes.

"Then we would head home for our Sunday dinner, our Sunday ritual."

I just sat and let Christine talk while I clasped my mug of coffee.

"After we had eaten, my father would say, 'Come on, let's leave your mother to her chores.' Then he would take me into the living room where he would lie down on his side on the settee. He would make me lie down in front of him.

"Then he would slip his hand up under my dress; he would pull me in tight against his body, his erection. I didn't know what it was back then, of course, but I was scared.

"I froze. I didn't dare to move. He would give me a little squeeze, pulling me in tighter, and gave this little wiggle. 'Let's get comfortable,' he said. I just laid there as still as I could be, with tears in my eyes, and wishing I could run away somewhere else, anywhere else.

We fell silent for a while. I didn't know what to say to that.

I sensed her pain and confusion, but I couldn't even begin to understand what she had gone through.

"I know this is going to sound strange to you, but some Sundays…"

I sat and waited.

"Some Sundays, when things were really bad, I would find myself looking down on these two people on the settee, and thinking, oh, that poor girl!"

65

Our estate wasn't a place where you would see much of your neighbours. But we could hardly have missed the two cat-crazy ladies directly across from us.

"Susie, Susie," Pat was calling out one evening, soon after we had moved in.

I opened the front door. "Is this who you are looking for?" I asked as Susie strolled casually out between my legs.

"What are you doing in there, you rascal," Pat asked.

"We had left our patio doors open," I explained. "I came down from upstairs, and there she was, making herself comfortable on our settee. I figured that she didn't live too far away."

"Well, what a little madam!" Pat exclaimed. "You must come over sometime soon and meet the other one. She doesn't travel nearly as far afield, but she must have gotten out and about somewhere. She is about ready to produce a litter, poor thing."

"I'm sure we would love to come and see them."

We started to become friends with the two of them. Kitten viewing over a cup of coffee and soon cat sitting for them while they were away for the weekend.

"Do you think they are gay?" Christine asked one evening after they had dropped off a thank-you gift of flowers.

"Of course they are, two attractive young women, living together in a one bedroom house," I answered.

"I don't think so," Christine continued, "they are just sharing the space to try and save money."

"I bet that they are gay, but it doesn't matter either way. They make nice neighbours."

Christine was sure that they were not gay. In fact, she was pretty sure back then that she was the only one in the whole world who had feelings for other women. But it peaked her interest, and she started to feel more relaxed about the idea that she might be gay.

Again, we shared thoughts and fantasies about women. Christine explored the idea of being with another woman from the safety of our home. I enjoyed the fantasies but feared the thought that one day she would find someone, and she would fall in love with her.

We had also talked from time to time about starting a family. The consensus was that one day when we could afford to raise children, we would go ahead and have perhaps two. Christine was young, and her biological clock hadn't started ticking quite yet.

In the meantime, I continued to enjoy photographing Christine. We no longer had the room to leave my make-do lights set up all of the time, but they were still there tucked into the back of the cupboard, and we had more freedom to go out and find locations to shoot in too.

But Christine also took it upon herself to find me a model or two. She would find a balance between discreetly hanging back out of the way and being forward enough to encourage the model. The occasional girl would feel more self-conscious about having another woman there seeing her in various states of undress, but for the most part, they felt reassured.

66

The conversations continued between us as to whether our neighbours Pat and Bev were gay or not. Christine remained certain that they were not but, in reality, she would benefit from knowing someone on a personal level that had come out as being gay. Even if it was only to very close friends.

We continued to visit, to cat sit, and to have dinners together at their house or ours. But they were not giving anything away. They would sit on our settee, one foot apart. Talk of work and where they had grown up, talk of cats of course, but little else. We for our part, we would never ask, of course.

Then one night our doorbell rang. It was Pat and Bev. "Come on in," we invited.

"We have something to tell you," Pat announced, "and well, we would rather you hear it from us first."

"Sit yourselves down," we prompted.

"We can't stay long," Pat continued. "It is just that your neighbours on that side have started spreading a rumour that we are gay. Yes, and well, we are; we just wanted you two to hear it from us first, instead of some gossip over the fence."

"Yes, so we always knew you were," we said almost in unison.

"Oh, good grief," Pat proclaimed, and suddenly the two of them were sat together as lovers, tangled at the end of our settee. "We didn't like to say anything."

"No and we didn't like to ask, but yes, we had assumed you were."

After that, we saw more of them, just two couples hanging out together. Then hearing that they liked to dance too, we took them along one night to one of our favourite clubs. We all went out on the floor and danced together, but they never felt that they could just be themselves. In that era, to be sure, it would have drawn some unwanted attention.

They couldn't invite me to go along to a club where they could dance and be themselves, so I said, "Perhaps you could take Christine along one night. She would be interested to see how the other half lives." We hadn't been too specific about exactly what those interests were, but I repeated, "Yes Christine would like to go, just to see what it is like, and to see you two enjoy yourselves."

The last thing I wanted to do was lose Christine, but Christine did need to find herself. To be comfortable in her own skin. So, off the three of them went one night, like a bunch of teenagers, to a gay club. I sat home, hoping at the very least that they would have fun.

A few hours later Christine announced, "It is not for me. Oh, Pat and Bev were great, and it was a fun night out. But the place wasn't very big, and it wasn't very busy, the women that were there were dykes. Butch, I don't know what to call them. There was no one there that I fancied."

"I am sorry that it wasn't a better night for you," I told her, and I knew that Christine would slip quietly back into her safe place, at least for a while.

67

I had become very well aware that I was not the centre of Christine's world, sexually at least. But we continued to grow closer together. For me, there was a degree of frustration when Christine was leaning towards her straight side. Yes, it was true she was unlikely to go running off with another woman, but she wasn't dealing with her troubled inner self.

In a way, a genie had been released from its bottle, and it was never going to be going back in. I very much wanted the real Christine to shine through, regardless of what that was going to mean for us. I wanted her to be happy. I wanted her to accept herself, whoever that was.

Neither of us had any specialist knowledge or experience with dealing with these problems. However, Christine was beginning to find the courage within herself to want to seek help. It was a huge step, a leap of faith and trust, when she found the strength to tell her doctor that she thought she might be gay.

Then for both of us, there was hope and apprehension. Her doctor referred her to a sexual therapist. Professional help. It was going to mean so much to both of us, but in particular to Christine, just to be on the road to recovery. There wasn't going to be an instant fix, but there was help out there.

The day arrived and off Christine went, visibly nervous. It was hard for me to concentrate on anything else. I spent the whole of the time while she was away, thinking about what she was going through, and hoping for the best for her.

An hour later, she breezed through the door, "Good news," she announced, "I am not gay."

I was in a state of instant bewilderment, "So what happened?" I asked. "What did she say?"

It turned out that this specialist asked Christine some very pointed questions about doing physical things to another woman, couched in some very crude terms.

"No," Christine answered.

"Then, of course, you are not gay," the sex therapist declared. "Get out of here."

So with that one single act of homophobia, the so-called specialist set Christine back years.

68

But all other aspects of our life continued to go well. We were enjoying our jobs and enjoying life in general. We had a reasonable amount of income and the stability we had always worked towards. Especially we were happy being together, so the question arose.

"Are we going to start a family sometime?"

"Sometime," Christine answered. "Why, what are your thoughts?"

"Well, we are never really going to be able to afford it," I said. "However, my job is going well, we could probably find a slightly bigger house when we need to."

"Yes, and?"

"Perhaps we should just stop trying not to have kids, and see what happens."

"Okay," Christine agreed.

So, Christine stopped taking the pill. We just got on with our lives and didn't think about it too much. The first few months when Christine's period arrived, we just put it down to the latent effect of the pills she had been taking for some years.

Then it started to become a disappointment to Christine. "Not this month," she'd announce. As time went on, we started to think about timing our lovemaking to increase the chances of Christine becoming pregnant. But still nothing.

One day out of the blue, a light went on in my head. The thought was suddenly there as a clear realisation. It was me. I couldn't have kids. I didn't know where it came from, except to say that I already knew that Christine could become pregnant.

"I am going to the doctors, to get myself checked out," I told Christine.

My doctor had me produce a specimen and sent it to the lab. Shortly after I was back in his office and he was telling me, "You have no sperm in your specimen, at all."

"You haven't had a vasectomy, have you?" But he already knew that the answer to that question was no.

"I want to send you in to see a urologist," he continued. "Get this checked out, as you could have a blockage."

Some months later I found myself walking through the door of the specialist's office.

Mr Meek looked up from his desk. "Hi," he called me by name. "How are you? What can I do for you? This is a surprise."

It was a surprise for me too. It had been years since I had worked for Mr Meek in the hospital service. I was flattered that he still remembered me. Then I shared my story.

"Okay, this is what we are going to do," Mr Meek started. "We will have you in, and I will do a bilateral biopsy of your testes, and at the same time, we will do an angiogram of the various tubes, just to see if there is a blockage in there somewhere. Hopefully, it is something simple, and we can fix this up for you."

I didn't care to think how painful this might be, but I agreed to go ahead with the procedure.

69

It was some time before any of this was going to happen. So we pretty much put it out of our heads, except perhaps on that day once a month when Christine's period would start. But by now we knew that we weren't going to be starting a family without my operation. So while it was still a bit of a disappointment, it wasn't unexpected.

Finally, the letter came through our letterbox. The date was set, and I booked some time off of work. I wasn't likely to feel too comfortable walking or even sitting for the first week or so. But this was what we needed to do. I had spent enough time in the operating theatres to know that this was pretty much routine, and so it was.

One minute an anaesthetist, who I had also worked with, was putting me to sleep and what seemed almost a moment later a nurse was waking me up. When they were sure that I was free from the effects of the anaesthetic they wheeled me back to the ward where I drifted in and out of sleep for the rest of the afternoon.

In the early evening I awoke to a hand resting on my arm. It was Mr Meek, my surgeon.

"Hi, how are you doing?" he asked me. "I thought that I would come around in person and tell you the news."

"Thank you," was about all I could offer through my still sleepy haze.

"There are no blockages, and everything looks perfectly normal," Mr Meek told me. "We will get the biopsy results, but I think we already know the answer to that," he continued. "You are never going to be able to have children of your own. I wish I could tell you why, but this is not something we normally see."

Somehow, I had prepared myself for this. It wasn't a total shock. "Thank you for all your time and effort, Mr Meek." But I found myself wishing I at least knew a reason. Perhaps it really was just one of those things.

"You take care of yourself now," Mr Meek added as he walked off.

Later when it was visiting hours, Christine sat on the side of the bed holding my hand. I told her the news. We were numb. There was nothing to be done about it. Accept our fate and move on. But I couldn't help but wonder, might Christine really want a family? If she did, she might want to start again with someone else.

70

"Here, take a look at this," I called to Christine.

It was Saturday morning, and I was sat nursing my second cup of coffee when I heard the mail arrive. Collecting it from the door I sat back down with my coffee, trying to make out this bright, colourful brochure that I was holding in my hand.

"A look at what?" Christine queried, descending the stairs and stepping into the lounge.

"Expo 86, in Vancouver, Canada. It says that we have been entered into a draw to win tickets."

"Where did they get your name and address?" Christine asked.

"I don't know. It says more details to follow. That will be interesting," I said, thinking aloud.

"That would be so nice, and we could go and see where you lived as a child," and with that, a seed was planted in Christine's brain.

"It would be an eight to ten-hour drive, but yes, we could see my hometown. Also, you would get to meet my uncles, aunts and cousins. I wonder," I added, "I'm betting it was my uncle that entered us into this draw."

"When is it on?" Christine asked.

"It runs right through the summer. Look, it is on for months."

I had always had this thought at the back of my head, someday it would be nice to get back and see the country of my birth, or at least the part of that country where I was born and where I lived until I was twelve. But being able to follow through on that thought, I couldn't see how I was ever going to be able to afford a trip like that.

Then, sure enough, more colourful brochures arrived. Yes, it was my uncle John that had entered us into the draw. My late mother's brother, the one who had spoiled me so as a kid. The uncle who had introduced me to electronics, just as my other uncle introduced me to photography.

"As you know, my uncle John runs his own television and radio repair shop, and I can't help wondering, if my father hadn't died, would I have ended up working for him?"

"You wouldn't want to live there though, would you?"

"No, not now; it is too small a town, but if we had never

left for England that might be exactly what I would have been doing. It would have been a very different sort of life," I added.

"I think I might have gone to Vancouver once. John and Madge were always taking me somewhere, while my poor sisters had to stay at home. They never had any children of their own, so I guess they enjoyed spoiling me. Then I think I vaguely remember swimming in the ocean somewhere. It was late and starting to get dark, and the three of us were in the water."

"If we win these tickets, the two of us can go and swim in the Pacific Ocean," Christine added for good measure.

71

"I got word at work today," I announced to Christine, "the contractors are being laid off."

"Good job you went full time then." She looked up at me for some reassurance.

"Yes, but I think that I might well be next. We have nearly completed this big order that has kept us busy these past couple of years, and I hear that there is nothing new on the books."

"What is that going to mean?" she asked.

"More travelling I think," I told her. "There is only one other firm around here doing any sort of electronics, and I won't be the only one looking for a job."

"Okay, get your CV out, let's get that up to date."

"Thank you, if you can type that up for me, that would be great. I will get some copies made, and I'm back to searching for a job."

One of my least favourite things, looking for a job, but then I have had a couple of years of experience in electronics to go with my City and Guilds. However, the one thing that my experience had shown me was what I didn't know. There were blanks in my understanding of how the circuits worked and even though I could usually tell whether they were working correctly or not, I think it would be helpful for me to learn some more. I wanted to have a deeper understanding of electronics.

"I looked in at the job centre today," I was telling Christine a few days later.

"Any luck there?" she asked.

"Nothing much there at all," I told her. "But," she stopped what she was doing and looked up, "they had a card up on the wall looking for people interested in taking the next level electronics course."

I paused, and she stood looking at me, waiting for more.

"I really think that I would be more employable with an Ordinary National Certificate in electronics."

"And?" Her one-word question left me uncertain as to what her reaction would be.

"I think that I should apply for it," I told her. "It would mean going off somewhere, another forty-six weeks. Are you willing to quit your job and come with me?"

"You mean that you haven't applied yet?"

So, the stage was set for another term in college for me. The timing was great. Soon after getting my notice at work, I received confirmation that I had been accepted on a course in the North of England. They found me a one bedroom furnished flat within an easy walking distance of the college, which I accepted sight unseen.

Christine handed in her notice at work, and we packed up the car ready for a new adventure.

72

I could have happily been a full-time academic. It was a small class with a good mixture of theory and practical work, and with my background, I found most of the material easy to understand. Then once I understood how something worked, there was no need to study. It wasn't going to be a big leap for me to get this qualification.

But there were some aspects of the course that were of added interest to me. The practical side, building a couple of circuits from scratch and testing them. Then the technical writing side. We were told that we were to produce a piece of technical writing that had to do with electronics. The choice of subject was ours, and we were given little information about what was expected, as to length or detail.

I had done some writing before, and it was something that I was interested in. I had also worked for ten years in the hospital service, and so it was an easy decision to write about medical electronics. Christine had her nurses training behind her, and she could touch type. She wasn't working or even looking for a job, and so I roped her in to do some of the research for me and all of the typing.

We had the whole of the course to complete this piece of technical writing. We just had to have something to hand in one month before the end of course. It wasn't a huge percentage of the marks for the course, but I realised it was an opportunity to produce something that might help me gain employment one day. So, the "Advent of Medical Electronics" was born.

Most of the class was ready to kill me the day I handed in a neatly bound manuscript, thirty-eight pages long, with an index and bibliography. One chap had, by contrast, four pages of handwritten notes.

"I didn't know we were supposed to do something like that," he said.

"Don't worry," I told him. "The whole thing is not worth many marks."

But I was secretly pleased with myself. I had enjoyed the project, I had learned from it, and I had something worth keeping. Perhaps even something to show during job interviews. Christine did all of the typing, but while we had the typewriter there, she started to teach me to touch type. Little did I know how valuable that would be to me in the future. Personal computers hadn't become a thing yet, but they weren't that far off.

So I was enjoying a stress-free life; the class was easy for the most part, and Christine was back at the flat cooking and looking after me. It was just a five-minute walk from the school, and so while most of the class was sat there with their sandwiches, I walked home for hot leftovers from the night before.

"You are not eating very much," I said to Christine one lunchtime. "What is wrong?"

"Nothing," she replied. "I'm just not very hungry."

"You have got to eat," I told her. It had dawned on me that several times recently, she hadn't been finishing her meals.

"I'm fine," she tried to reassure me, but by the way she turned away, I started to have the feeling she wasn't fine.

"Come on, sit down and eat," I insisted. "I am not going back to class until I see that you have eaten a reasonable lunch."

So I monitored her food intake because she had started to worry me. I had absolutely no idea that by the time I was halfway back to school, she had been into the bathroom and made herself sick. Fingers down her throat; I had never even heard of anorexia, let alone bulimia. She seemed overly slim, but I saw that she was eating a reasonable meal each day.

73

Life wasn't all about study and writing, sitting in at night and watching television. Money was tight, even more so than the previous course. We had a mortgage to pay, and we were starting to get behind with that. But we needed something to do with ourselves on weekends.

Not too far a walk away from us was a nightclub. A

reasonable dance floor, not too crowded, and the music was good for the most part. The biggest draw was that if we arrived early, admission was free. Not only that, but it was happy hour. Two double whiskies and ginger ale for a quid, in a tall glass with a little ice. We would take our two drinks each and find a table with a good view of the arriving crowd.

We would sit and talk, enjoy our drinks, but most of all we would people watch. In fact, in reality, we would 'girl watch'.

"What was she thinking wearing that?" Christine would ask.

"I think that she might have wanted to practice walking in those heels," I would add.

Sometimes the door would open, and if I were looking elsewhere, I would feel a squeeze of my hand. I would know to look up, then a little nod from Christine would point me in the right direction. Sometimes to something bizarre but almost always to a beautiful young woman. Strikingly lovely.

"I would love to be photographing her," I might remark.

"Only if I can come and hold the reflector," Christine might say.

Then someone might catch my eye, and I would attract Christine's attention. "I am in lust," I would whisper in Christine's ear.

"I am in lust too," Christine would reply. "What I wouldn't want to do with her!"

"I think that it is time we went out and did some dancing," I might say and lead Christine out onto the floor. Once our drinks were empty, we almost never went back to the bar, not after happy hour was over. We would spend most of the rest of the night out on the dance floor. Enjoying the music, moving to the beat, having fun and enjoying each other's company.

Then whenever Christine felt this free to express her interest in girls, she also felt freer to enjoy her sex life. We could both fantasise about the woman we saw. Or someone we had been attracted to. Christine felt safe to openly wonder what it would be like to be sharing the bed with another woman, instead of me.

And for a while, at least we were close to having the free and easy sex life we had enjoyed in the early days of our relationship. For me it was a mixed blessing, this brought us ever closer together but at the same time I had to realise Christine was in all probability gay. One day I was going to lose her to another woman.

But for my part, whilst I would have loved the excitement of a fling with any one of these girls, they would never be a replacement for Christine.

74

Eighty-five percent was a good pass mark, and I was pleased with myself. Pleased and ready to job hunt in the hope of finding an even better job. Expo 86 was over, but it was still there in our minds, or Christine's mind at least.

"I really want us to move to Canada," Christine announced.

"What about your parents?" I asked. "What are they going to have to say about that?"

"They are just going to have to get used to it," she declared. "We haven't seen much of them while we have been up here. Please," she added, "will you find out what is involved?"

"Okay, we can go up to Canada House in London as soon as we get back," I offered.

We were going to have to move anyway. It had always been in the back of my mind to go and live in the country of my birth, but wow! House prices had been going up really fast, and perhaps that would give us the leverage to make such a major move.

I was a little surprised that Christine was so keen to be moving so very far away and leaving her parents behind. For my part, both of my parents had passed on, and so it would just be my sisters and my stepfather. My sisters were born there too, so perhaps they would want to come and visit.

Then like a snowball that had started rolling down a hill, momentum started to build, and there was no stopping now. I sent for copies of the local papers to begin job hunting. I was surprised, shocked even, when turning straight to the job section I found nothing in the electronics field.

"There must be electronics there," I announced.

"Perhaps you will have to go to the local job centre," Christine decided.

We made the trip to London and started things moving; we filled out the forms for Christine's immigration papers.

"Okay we can start them here, but you must go back to Canada and re-establish residency before you can complete the process and get legal status for your wife," they told us.

"But I can take her there on holiday with me, and do the paperwork, can't I?" I asked.

"Yes, you can do it that way. Your wife just won't be able to work until the paperwork is complete," they told us.

I was a little surprised that it wasn't easier than that, but it could work. So, our plan continued; we would get ourselves over there, and I would start job hunting right away. We would then do the rest of the paperwork as soon as we could, and I would support us until Christine's papers come through. This was not going to be a problem. We were on the train heading home and trying to make sense of it all.

"I guess that the next step is to put the house on the market," suggested Christine.

"Yes," I agreed. "That is the only way we can do this, so I hope that we can get a good price."

"How long do you think it will take to sell?" Christine asked.

"Good question," I told her. "We could be sitting on this for months, waiting for the right buyer."

"Oh, I hope not," she said. "I hope not."

"Well, we will contact someone and get it listed," I said. "Then at least we will have some idea of what we will be dealing with money wise."

75

For my part, I was dragging my heels. Yes, it had always been a dream of mine to go back to live and work in Canada. But that is just what it was, a dream. I didn't have an adventurous gene in my whole body. For the most part, I was happy with the status quo, oh, and to make matters worse, I had a fear of flying! No reason for it, it made no logical sense, but it was there.

So if this had all fallen apart, I might have been secretly relieved. There was so much to do, and so many things that could have got in the way. We had to sell the house and have enough money left over after paying off the mortgage to make this trip, with enough cash in our pockets to support ourselves while we found work. We would have to sell the furniture, it would not make sense to try and take that all with us.

We had to pack up everything that we really wanted to keep; everything that we would want to have with us in our new lives. Then arrange some way of having it sent over to us, should we find work and decide to settle there. We had to find some way of storing it in the meantime, long term, in case we didn't find work or didn't like it there. We may even have become homesick.

But the realtor told us how much we could expect to get for our little one bedroom house, and yes, it was going to be enough. She also told us that she thought that it would sell reasonably easily. A month, maybe two at the most. That was good news; it would give us time to get ourselves organised. I was glad to have some extra time on my hands.

Christine, for her part, could have been packed and ready to go within a day or two. She had been the driving force behind this, ever since that first brochure came through the letterbox. Yes, she was my life. Ever since the very first days of our relationship. Now I was going to find a way to overcome my fears and be on that plane beside her.

So sometimes, no matter how hard you try, things don't work out for you. But sometimes it seems that things are meant to be. Within ten days we had a message that our realtor thought that they had a buyer for our house. He was coming back for a second look. Then later that day we heard, yes, he wants to buy. Also, he had asked, "would we be willing to sell all of the furniture for an extra sum."

"Yes, certainly," we told them. The idea of having to advertise and sell each piece of furniture separately did not appeal; we would still be living in the place while, bit by bit, things move out to their new homes, perhaps sleeping on the floor, or having to sit on cardboard boxes. This way we had the use of everything until the day we moved out. Then all we would have to do is to pack up our last few things and walk out of the door.

My stepfather told us how utterly stupid we were being to move to Canada, and what a disaster it would be. But he agreed to put us up from the time we closed on our house until the day we flew off. He also agreed to store our boxes and trunks, full of all the things we really didn't want to part with or thought that we could use in our new home.

The day arrived, we were homeless and ready to go. Christine was very patient with me. I was packed and fully committed to going, but my fear of flying wasn't even allowing me to book the tickets. My doctor was very understanding and put me on pills to ease my anxiety. They helped, but the sessions of hypnotherapy, well I don't think they did anything other than to highlight the fact that I was anguished.

Ten hours in a plane, ten hours with no control over my own fate. It wasn't the flying, it wasn't the height, it was purely that lack of control. Putting my life in the hands of another. Every single day that I waited there were thousands of safe flights crossing back and forth across the Atlantic and everywhere else you could think of. But knowing that didn't really help.

Then I discovered a deal. Greyhound was offering two-week travel anywhere in North America for just ninety-nine pounds. I could fly to Toronto, five hours in the air, then we could check out that area and the job prospects before making our way across to the West Coast. Christine would discover just how vast that continent really is.

It really didn't make any sense, but if it got me on that plane, it would have to do.

76

It took quite a while, but finally, there I was airborne. Sleeping for most of the journey or otherwise out of it. However, all of my nerves were about making that commitment, once I was up there I relaxed. My fate is in the hands of the gods of the air. So five hours on, Christine and I are looking out of the window. We are descending down past the CN Tower and into Toronto. It was twenty-seven years since I was last in Canada.

Down on the ground and safely installed in our hotel, we could have crashed from the jet lag, but instead, we were excited and ready to explore. The idea that there might be more jobs in Toronto went straight out of the window. We were on holiday, and we may never be back this way, so let's play the tourist was what we decided.

Niagara Falls was not so far away, and so that was the top of our must-see list. We hired a car, and I drove us down. The falls themselves were spectacular, but I immediately noticed the lack of scenery along the way. The area seemed so flat and

boring, not the Canada I remembered as a child. The lake was
so huge; you wouldn't even know that it is a lake. Yes, it had a
pleasant beach, but there was nothing that was going to sell us
on the area itself.

Fleetwood Mac was about to play at Maple Leaf Gardens,
and so we stayed a couple of days to take in the concert. I felt
it was a good omen, to finally see that concert with Christine.
Then we packed our bags to head off on the long overland
journey by Greyhound bus.

The plan was to travel for as long as we could stand to be
travelling, cooped up in a bus. Then we would stop overnight
for a break, or stop anywhere that really took our interest. So,
we headed south and crossed the border into the United States,
the first visit for Christine. I had never been to that area before,
and so it might as well have been a first for me too.

"Let's make Chicago our first stopover," I suggested.

"That sounds good," Christine said. "We could have
watched the Chicago Bears play live, but it is a long way to
the weekend, and even then, we don't know if they would be
playing at home or away."

"Well, one day perhaps." We had watched American
football on television so many times in the past few years.

Soon we were off the bus, and we found a locker large
enough to leave our luggage in for the day. We were ready
to set off on our adventure, but as we were about to exit the
bus station, a ruckus caught our attention. There inside the
bus stop canteen, a very large black policeman was beating on
a ragged-looking black man with his truncheon. Not a very
good first impression.

Once outside we headed down to what appeared to be the
main drag and into a howling wind. It was still October, but it
was cold and unpleasant. We didn't get very far before we were
asking ourselves whether we really wanted to be doing this.

"We could really do with a holdall or something to carry

onto the bus with us," Christine declared. "I suggest that we pop into the nearest department store, treat ourselves to a carry-on, and get back on the next Greyhound out of here."

"That sounds like a really good plan," I agreed.

St. Louis proved a much more amiable stopping-off point. It was the year that they won the World Series. The city was abuzz with the excitement, and everyone was friendly. It was a welcome break, and we were sure glad to have a comfortable bed for the night. A refreshing shower and a change of clothes. Then the big highlight, a stop in a launderette! Repacked our cases, and we were ready for the road again.

77

It was a long trip with ever-changing scenery. The inner cities may have all been similar, but the countryside changed radically along the way. There was big sky country, and you could almost see the cowboys driving a herd of cattle across the open plains. Then there were the Rocky Mountains, and most of it was going to be in the dark.

"But we will go back, and you will see them in the daylight," I promised.

"And now here we are almost directly below the area in British Columbia where I was born. We will go there too, sometime soon," I continued. "Even if we decide to go back to England."

There we were in Washington State, in areas I had visited as a child. Even though I had been too young to remember most of it. We used to drop down across the border and into Spokane, I remembered that, and I remembered the scenery. Vast areas of evergreen forest and mountainous rocky outcrops. I was beginning to feel at home.

One more brief stop in Seattle, a change of bus, and we were off north again, heading up to Vancouver, crossing the border and counting down the final miles. How far had we come? How many days? Ten or so including stopovers. Ten days of travel instead of ten hours in the air. Still, we had some idea of where we were and just how vast North America really is.

Then road weary and tired, we were in Vancouver. We had pre-booked three nights at the YWCA, and we were glad of the time to sort ourselves out and get our bearings. Laundry is done, fresh, clean clothes and a shower every day. Luxury, and not having to be on the move all the time. For whatever was ahead of us we had three months before our return tickets would expire.

So what next? We asked at the desk. I was shocked at how much they wanted for us to stay one full week. I thought that this place was supposed to be reasonable.

"Let's go and explore," Christine said. "Let's see what we can find."

"At their rates, we will be broke long before we can find our feet," I added.

We set off down the road, keeping our eyes peeled for possibilities. Not really knowing our way around or just where we were, only that it was the downtown core.

"There are two big department stores, but you know, there doesn't seem to be much else, are we missing something?" I asked.

"There must be more stores than this," Christine stated. "This is a major city."

"Let's head down here."

We were walking down a street of high fashion stores. Name brand places that you would recognise anywhere. Fancy outfits and then fancy shoes to go with them. Then restaurants and pizza places and suddenly it is not looking quite so posh anymore.

"Let's ask in here," Christine suggested.

There was a reasonable looking restaurant taking up most of the base of a high-rise hotel. A large revolving sign announcing both the restaurant and the hotel. There was a vacancy sign, under the plaque naming the hotel. Suites are available, it told us. It was the end of October, and so I'd guess the end of their summer holiday season.

"There is no harm in asking," I said.

Inside, there was a pleasant surprise waiting for us. For a little more than the price we had been quoted for a one-week stay earlier that day, we could have a suite here for the whole month.

"Can we see one of the suites, please?" I was still a little sceptical.

"Sure, come on up," said the man behind the desk. "Do you have a car?" he asked. "There is not much parking. There's a swimming pool in the basement, open all year round; just ask for the key at the front desk. Here we go," he said, as the elevator arrived.

The room was basic, but clean and well looked after. There was a small lounge area with a kitchen off to one side. A separate bedroom and an adequate bathroom.

"If you are renting by the month the cleaner comes in weekly and changes the bed linen and your towels," the desk clerk told us. "Local calls are free, as are the regular TV channels."

"We would just have to pick up some dishes and pots and pans," Christine stated, looking at me.

"Oh, we have a store of them you can use," the clerk offered.

"We will take it," I told him, with a nod to Christine.

78

We were right there on Robson Street, the Rodeo Drive of Vancouver. It was bright and vibrant. The first few days of November and the sky was blue. Short sleeves were almost enough for most of the day. You might want a jacket in the evening or some sort of wrap, but on the whole, it was very comfortable.

We shopped at the local supermarket, a short walk down the road. Soon we had stocked our fridge and cupboards, but it really didn't matter what time of day it was. If you run out of something, or if you have forgotten something, there was an open shop close by. There was a market even closer than the supermarket, with fresh vegetables and fish and meat in abundance.

Then we started to discover the area. On three sides, we were surrounded by water. There was a seawall framing the huge Stanley Park, with its pathway leading you around in almost a circle. There were sandy beaches along the south side. To the north, there was the inner harbour, with seaplanes landing. Expensive looking yachts. A sea bus crossing back and forth to the North Shore.

There were street cafes with people sitting out relaxing, enjoying their coffees, enjoying the popular sport of 'people watching'. Two men walked by hand in hand, and well, quite honestly, no one really took any notice. We found our bearings, and we found ourselves to be feeling comfortably at home in no time at all.

Our hotel was mainly used by tourists through the summer months, it had a wall full of brochures of local attractions. These were a starting point for us as we came to know our new city. Stanley Park was right there, almost on our doorstep. One hundred years previous, Lord Stanley had the foresight to create a beautiful park, right there in the city. Acres of woodland left untouched except for the footpaths that ran through it. It included a large grassed area with an open-air theatre, plus an aquarium with a small petting zoo for the children.

There were picnic tables with benches for the public's use, but some people just threw a blanket on the ground and enjoyed their meal. Then there was the mini railway, a station where they picked up passengers on a journey around some of the larger animals in the zoo area. But the rail line was surrounded by a footpath, and we chose to walk the loop.

These were the first of a few pleasant surprises. Pony rides for the kids. A wooden fence enclosed a circular path where, for a small fee, a child could get their first experience of horse riding. I suddenly had a memory of having taken just such a ride as a child, travelling with my uncle and aunt. My pony took the shortest possible route, and I remember scratch marks on my leg from rubbing up against the fence.

We rounded a corner to find a couple feeding squirrels. A gentleman stood with a bag of nuts in his hand, and a squirrel had climbed his trouser leg and was tugging at his sleeve. We stood watching for a while, and soon we had squirrels at our feet, looking up at our empty hands.

"Next time, we'll bring nuts," we told them.

Around the next corner, we were even more amazed. People stood near a large area of bushes with their hands held out. We stopped and watched as little chickadees flew down and landed on their hands, helping themselves to the offering of sunflower seeds.

I looked across at Christine.

"I don't want to have to go back to England," she announced. "This is where I want to live."

"We had better find ourselves some jobs," I told her. I couldn't help but smile at the simple joys that were selling her on this new place.

79

Finding work, and finding it in time before our returns tickets expired and our money ran out, that was going to be our biggest hurdle. Christine couldn't even start job hunting until we finished her paperwork and she had her landed immigrant status. That could take a couple of months, and to top it off, she was supposed to fly back to England and her parents, to collect her papers.

I could job hunt straight away, except that I, having lived outside the country since I was twelve, had never been issued my paperwork. But that first hurdle was cleared easily enough with a visit to the job centre. So my paperwork was on the way, but there was not one single electronics job posted on the walls anywhere. There must be electronics here, I thought to myself. So, I asked at the desk.

"No, companies like that would never post a vacancy here."

"So how do I find work in my field," I asked somewhat bewildered.

"You will have to go and drop your resume off at any company that you would like to work for."

That was completely crazy, I thought to myself. I wanted a job and as long as it is electronics I really didn't care what it was that they're making. But that is the way it works here, and so I started to gather a list of company names and addresses, photocopied a bunch of resumes and started to drop them off. Places I had never heard of, and at addresses I had never seen before.

I did, however, find a job doing telephone surveys part time. The least rewarding thing that I had ever done. But there was a little bit of money coming in each week, and it was already clear that it would likely be very close. We could be out of money long before the date on our return tickets.

So, we got ourselves into the immigration office and finished up the paperwork for Christine. It was a formality, but that didn't mean that it would happen in a hurry.

"I think that is everything we need," the clerk told us. "I will just take this out and have my supervisor look over it. You realise that you have to sponsor your wife for her first ten years in Canada?"

I nodded, yes, as the clerk walked off with the paperwork.

In the next booth, a couple of landed immigrants and now citizens were asking about sponsoring their nephew into the country.

"Yes, now that you are citizens, you can do that. You will have to agree to sponsor him for three full years."

I couldn't say a word for fear that I might somehow delay Christine's paperwork.

We just had to hope that it would come through in good time for Christine to start her job search before the date on our return tickets.

80

I had told my relatives, some five hundred miles inland in my hometown, that we were there in Vancouver. I fully expected an invitation to visit. In fact, I had expected an invitation to come for Christmas. But we had heard nothing, and so we decided that, as this could well be our only Christmas ever in Canada, we were going to have a proper Christmas.

Just down the road, a man was selling Christmas trees in this empty lot. We bought the smallest one he had there. Then we got a few little decorations and some paper streamers to try to make it look festive. It was the poorest, barest Christmas tree I had ever seen. But we would make the best of it.

Frozen turkeys were cheaper than fresh ones, but they would take some time to defrost. Our fridge had a tiny freezer compartment, no room for more than a couple of bags of vegetables. We bought the smallest bird we could find and set it out on the draining board. We were all set; we could get the vegetables and condiments any time in the week.

A small package arrived along with a Christmas card from Christine's parents. "What is this that they have sent," Christine asked out loud, as she opened the card. "Thinking of you at Christmas," it read. Then she opened the Christmas present. Two cheap yellow pillow cases probably picked up in a thrift shop. Christine sat there and cried. "They are not even a colour we might use," she said.

It wasn't looking as if it would be much of a Christmas. But then the phone rang. I was sure that it must be the reception desk downstairs. We didn't know anyone here that might call us.

"Hello," I answered.

"You guys are coming out for Christmas, aren't you?" It was my uncle.

"Oh, I hadn't heard anything, I didn't know if we were invited," I offered.

"Of course, you are invited," he told me. "I am expecting you."

"I will check in with Greyhound today and see about tickets," I told him, all the time thinking to myself, I wish we hadn't bought that turkey. But I was pleased and relieved and suddenly looking forward to my first Christmas in my hometown in twenty-eight years.

"There will be snow, and it will be cold," I told Christine. "We will need to get ourselves some winter coats to wear."

We set off to buy bus tickets, and then to a department store to get the warmest, cheapest winter coats we could find. Bright yellow, and we would stand out like a sore thumb, but the price was right. We didn't know then, but they would stand us in good stead as we stood at the side of the Columbia River less than a week later. It was minus sixteen with a wind blowing.

We pulled one of the shelves out of the fridge to make room for the turkey, in the hopes that it would still be good to cook when we got back.

My uncle was the classic boy who never grew up. Oh, he was mature, but he never lost his innocence, and he never lost his sense of fun. Christine immediately felt at ease when she met him, and he took us around the local area, giving Christine a sense of what life was like for me when I was young.

"Where would you like to go today?" he asked.

"I don't know," Christine told him. "I don't know the area."

"Would you like to drive out to the lake?" he continued.

It was Christmas week.

"How far is it," Christine asked.

"Oh, it is just around the corner," he told her.

It was twenty-five miles away. But for him that was nothing. The scenery was beautiful, white snow on the ground and blue skies. Evergreen trees and a display of frost and crystals in the shaded areas.

The general store and coffee shop were closed. The campground was empty, but you could get a sense of what it would be like in summer.

"You can drive back," my uncle announced, passing the keys to Christine.

"No, I can't drive, I don't have a licence," Christine recoiled.

I drove back instead.

81

January arrived, and we were back at our hotel, eating a seemingly endless supply of turkey. It was a new year, a new life, we were optimistic. All we needed was a decent job, but Christine's papers hadn't come through yet, and I wasn't getting any response from any of the resumes that I had dropped off.

"This is where I want to live," Christine reminded me, yet again.

"We will get there," I reassured her, but I was concerned about my lack of job prospects.

Still, Christine was totally at home here. There was something about her that was more relaxed. I couldn't quite put my finger on it, but somehow this is where we belonged.

It was winter, and yes you needed a coat, but for the most part, the sky was blue, and it was inviting outside. There was always somewhere to explore.

The indoor hotel pool was open year-round. We would pick up the key from reception and take a swim. The pool was always ours; we never had any company down there. There were no windows that looked in. Then one day we were flirting in the water.

"I could go and accidentally lock the door," I told Christine one afternoon.

We made love in the pool, totally undisturbed. It was just one part of a more relaxed, open-minded Christine. She never froze in bed. We talked about girls. We fantasised, and we talked about her exploring her sexuality. She wasn't ready for that in the cold light of day, but in the warmth and security of our bed, I was reminded that there was a strong chance that I would lose her to another woman.

In the meantime, I enjoyed sharing this new-found openness. For my part, I knew that I would be more than happy to be sharing Christine with another woman, or even sharing another woman with Christine. Christine, however, still had the sense that she was the only women in the world that felt sexually attracted to other women.

But at least she felt safe enough with me to tug on my hand and point out passing beauties. Or whisper in my ear saying, "Look over there, coming through the door."

Then there were girls walking hand in hand or flirting in public places, especially as we discovered Davie Street. Some cafes and restaurants were obviously dedicated to their gay clientele, and whether it was breakfast or a late-night meal, they were well supported.

There were a couple of nightclubs in this area and from the queues outside they were gay too. Then there was the bookshop, Little Sisters and well, it would take a while, but with my support, Christine would be finding a whole new world of reading material.

82

"I don't want to have to go home to pick up my immigration papers," Christine announced one day.

"We did kind of promise your parents you would," I reminded her. They hadn't arrived yet, but it was about the time that we had been told they should be ready.

"I wish that we could just have them arrive here, and I could just get on and job hunt."

"You know that you have to arrive at customs with them to complete the process," I offered.

"I know," Christine replied.

I hadn't seen Christine looking down or feeling blue for a single moment since we arrived. I had somehow thought that she would have relished sharing details of her adventure so far with them. Yes, it didn't make any sense spending that money to send her back, let alone take up valuable job-hunting time being away in England.

Then we had a timely break. Air Canada went on strike, and suddenly there was a shortage of seats on flights across the Atlantic. The price of fares soared. We couldn't have afforded those rates even if we had wanted to.

We explained the situation to Christine's parents as best we could in a letter, and they agreed to send her papers to us by secure courier as soon as they arrived.

Christine was relieved at not having to go home to pick them up, and I was relieved at not having to spend the extra money right now. It was going to be tight as it was. I had not had a single response from any of the resumes that I had put out there, and I was running out of companies to try. Every electronics company within one hour on public transit had one of my resumes.

So, the moment that the paperwork arrived we hired a car,

and I drove Christine down across the border into the United States, just to turn around and drive back to Canada Customs. It was just a formality, and we were soon on our way again, with a landed immigrant stamp in Christine's British passport.

The next day we were at the job centre, getting the rest of the paperwork completed for Christine's Social Insurance Number, and now, at last, she could start job hunting. But the date was quickly approaching for our return airline tickets; tickets we didn't ever want to use, but we desperately needed that option. Neither of us had any access to social security in Canada, but we both did in England.

We had already taken a big chance and spent several hundred dollars on extending the dates of our return flights by one month. Now both of us had to job search in earnest.

"Okay, this is it. If one of us gets a full-time job before this date, we will stay. Otherwise, we fly home," I looked to Christine for her agreement.

"I am sure that we can do this." She didn't look quite as sure as she sounded.

I still had my part-time telephone survey job, but it wasn't regular, and it didn't give me nearly enough hours of work a month. There were other jobs that I had applied for, but the usual response was that I was overqualified and that they believed I would not stay.

83

"I have a full-time job," Christine announced, after several false starts. "I start Monday morning."

I still didn't seem any closer to finding something myself.

"Great news," I congratulated her. "What is it; even more important, where is it?"

"Just a short ride on the SkyTrain," she declared. "Thank goodness for the SkyTrain."

"Easy to get to, that is great."

"It is a medical aid supply company," she continued.

"We can stay," I offered. I don't know how we would ever have got ourselves on that flight back to England. Christine was to start a full-time job on Monday, and our return tickets were for the Wednesday. We were cutting it far too close for comfort.

We had a little celebratory dinner that weekend. Relieved, pleased with ourselves, optimistic. There was little money left to eat out, but we made something special for ourselves in our hotel room, and we treated ourselves to a cheap bottle of wine.

"A toast to Christine," I offered, knowing that on my own I would not have the chance to stay.

So, on Monday morning, Christine went off to work, and I job searched with new vigour. Now I have to find something, anything, just to get some income going.

I was there waiting as Christine walked through the door that evening. She was in tears. I held her, and she sobbed on my shoulder.

"What is it?" I asked her.

"It was horrible," she answered between sobs. "They are not nice people at all."

"I am sorry," I told her. "Well, we can pack our bags and catch that flight on Wednesday."

"No, I want to stay. I will stick it out until you find a full-time job, and then I will find something different."

"Are you sure?" I asked.

"Yes," she was adamant.

So, the next morning Christine went off to work. That night she declared that it was not good, but that she would cope. "Are you sure?" I asked her. "We could fly home tomorrow."

But she was determined to stay, whatever it was going to take. So then Wednesday morning she went off to work again, and we let our airline tickets expire. We were staying in Canada.

The first week went by, and she assured me that she was getting used to it, to them. By the next Thursday, it was to be her first payday, and just in time because we had enough money left to pay next month's rent, but nothing left over to feed ourselves. Far too close for comfort.

Then Thursday afternoon Christine arrived back from work early.

"What's up?" I asked. "I wasn't expecting you quite so soon."

There was a look of shock on her face.

"They called me into the office about an hour before quitting time. I just thought that they were going to give me my pay. Instead, they told me that they are going bankrupt and that they cannot afford to pay me, and that I might as well go home."

"We have stayed here on the strength of that job; did they know that?" I asked flabbergasted. "They still have to pay you for your work," I added, thinking out loud.

Somehow I knew that there were employment standards people, and I had the good sense to phone them. They told us to both go in together on Monday and let them know that we have spoken to employment standards personnel. Tell them that they have two weeks to pay up, and then after that, if they haven't paid us, they would take it up with them on our behalf.

So that is just what we did.

84

In the meantime, Christine poured over the job sections of both the local papers and circled anything even remotely interesting. There wasn't a lot in there, but there were possibilities. Then Monday morning she was on the phone, and out dropping off resumes.

It had been a very worrying weekend, and the worry continued into Monday. But Monday afternoon Christine announced that she had a job interview on that Tuesday morning. A little ray of hope and I was back out dropping off resumes, all to places I had been before. Staying optimistic was tough. I visited the job centre, for what it was worth. Trying to find something, anything full time. Stocking shelves or sweeping floors, I would have done anything I could to bring in a paycheque.

Tuesday morning Christine was downtown at her job interview, while I sat nervously back in our hotel suite. It seemed to be taking a very long time or was that just me. It must be a good sign, I was telling myself. Surely, she should be back by now. Then the phone rang.

"Hello."

"It's me," Christine's voice announced. "They have asked me to start right away, so I am just going to grab a sandwich and then off to work."

"Excellent, congratulations," I offered.

You could hear the relief in both of our voices.

"I will be home soon after five," Christine continued. "I will tell you all about it then."

"I will look forward to it," I told her. "In the meantime, I will be out dropping off resumes, but I will be home before you, I am sure."

This had all been far tougher than either of us had imagined. Somehow, we had thought that it would just be an extension of England. An English-speaking Commonwealth country, why should anything be much different? But it was.

I had managed to have a couple of interviews at this point. I would show up very neatly groomed in a smart two-piece suit. White shirt and tie. Briefcase under my arm with my references, qualifications, and a few extra resumes. Just as I would have expected to do in the Old Country.

The guy doing the interview was sat there in jeans and a tee shirt. He was polite. A nice firm handshake, but then he proceeded to ask what my qualifications meant, and how did they relate to a local electronics course that I had never heard of.

"You are overqualified," I would be told.

"I am sorry, but this job would just bore you; you have too much experience." Or various versions of the same thing.

I needed a break, a little bit of luck, anything to get me started. It was another couple of weeks, but I returned to a small company that I had left a resume at before. "Just a minute," the receptionist said, and she disappeared through the old grey door.

"Take a seat," she told me on her return. "Someone will see you in a few minutes."

So, there I was, sitting and talking to an Englishman, who knew and appreciated the difficulties that I was experiencing. He also knew what my qualifications meant.

"I don't have any test engineer jobs, but I do need someone in assembly," he told me. "The job is yours if you want it."

85

It was a major relief. We were both working full time. Not on the best wages we had ever earned, but enough to pay the rent and feed ourselves each month. I had a brief moment to relax before Christine suggested it might be time to start looking for our own flat.

We didn't have a stick of furniture to our names. There were two steaming trunks and three tea chests full of our personal items waiting to be shipped out to us, but that was it. We were going to need these things to get us started in a flat, but we couldn't get them shipped until we actually had an address to send them to.

So yes, we were going to want our own place, and yes it would be cheaper than the hotel suite. But we would need our rent deposit, something to sleep on, some bedding, something to cook with. It would be a long time before we could afford our own transport, and so we would both want to be within walking distance of our work.

I was thinking somewhere just outside of the main downtown core. A little farther to walk yes, but a little less expensive. However, Christine had her mind made up. She had found, she announced, a clean, well-maintained block of flats, just two blocks from the beach.

"Look, they have a launderette right inside the building." Christine was excited. "It even has a balcony, we can sit outside in the evening," she continued.

"Okay, we can go and look." I caved in easily.

I would have happily stayed where we were until we had a little money saved up. But Christine said, "I will sleep on the floor if I have to."

With both of us having just started new jobs, both still within our probation periods, and with no local history of having rented before, we applied to rent the apartment. We didn't even have a local reference to give, but we were accepted!

Christine was over the moon with delight. I was happy, but at the same time I was wondering, how in the world are we going to make this work?

There were blinds on the windows, a reasonable stove, and a fridge with a freezer unit on the top, which was larger than anything we had in England. There was carpet on the floor, and all things considered, it was very much better than the flat that we had lived in when we were first together. There was an endless supply of running hot water, and the electricity was included in the rent.

We bought ourselves a fold-down futon that became our double bed at night and arranged for it to be delivered the day we got the keys. Christine found a beat up, old coffee table, abandoned by the dumpster. Plus, high praise for the local Canadian Tire store where we found a cheap set of plates, cutlery, and saucepans. Plus, a couple of towels, two sheets, and a duvet.

We were set. We had prepaid the shipping on our goods from England, and we sent for them. We ate off of our laps, and we watched the weather changing outside of our window for entertainment. We had glorious walks within easy reach, and our bright yellow coats to keep us warm whatever the weather did.

We were happy. Now that the stress of being out of work had passed, now that we both had an income, even living with just the basics, we were happy. There was an exciting road of opportunities laid out in front of us, a beautiful city to explore, and it was going to take time to gather a life around ourselves, but it was going to be a joyful adventure.

86

It was idyllic. Work was close by; Christine walked, while I took a little water ferry across the inlet called False Creek. We discovered Granville Island, there on the same short ferry ride that I took to work each day. We would shop there some weekends, choosing from the huge selection of fresh fruits and vegetables. There was a butcher shop with a vast array of fresh meats and a bakery full of hard-to-resist bread and cakes.

We became members of the Aquarium, where we enjoyed viewing the tanks of tropic sea life as well as the amazingly colourful specimens from the local coast. But it was the orcas that really captured our hearts and our imagination. Standing by the underground viewing windows and watching this massive creature swim by, or sitting up on the deck at feeding time and seeing the same whale leave the water completely only to splash down seconds later and soak some of the visitors in the front row seats.

Sometimes we would walk into Stanley Park with our bag of nuts and a handful of sunflower seeds. We fed the squirrels. The boldest of them would climb our trouser legs to take the nuts right out of our hands. Then it was on to the bushes where the little chickadees would gather. They seemed almost weightless as they landed, so very briefly, on our hands to collect our offering of a single sunflower seed.

We started to discover live theatre very close by. Steel Magnolias performed live on stage. We had seen the film version but hadn't realised it had also become a play. Then there was the stage version of Dangerous Liaisons. But even without spending cash on a ticket, there were buskers to entertain you playing their music along the seawall. There were artists displaying and offering their artwork for sale, and as always there was 'people watching'.

We found out about the Georgia Straight, the alternative press delivered free to the entrance lobby of our building. If it wasn't there, it would be available in countless outlets nearby. It was supported by its many adverts for all of those things you never knew that you needed. It was full of stories the mainline press would never cover, even alternate points of view. But then it was also full of local events, meetings, bands playing and show openings.

Plus of course, the personal ads, most notably 'Woman Seeking Woman'. Christine could no longer think that she was the only woman in the world that was attracted to other woman. You only had to step outside our front door. Two blocks away the nearest restaurants catered to the gay community and the nearest three night clubs were gay.

While Christine wasn't ready to pursue a different lifestyle, she was boosted by the thought that she wasn't alone in her feelings and the fantasies that she was always lead to believe were outside of the norm. She could now not worry about the homophobic advice that she had always been given every time she had summoned the courage to seek help. Here there was hope that she wouldn't be totally ostracised for the mere act of expressing her feelings.

I was in over my head. All of this was completely foreign to me, but I did what I could to support Christine and let her know that she was loved. I, being a healthy heterosexual male, couldn't help but be interested in the idea of sharing another woman with Christine.

By now I had come to realise that Christine was more interested in other girls than she was in other men or me. So, I could only foresee two likely outcomes. The most likely being that I would one day lose her to another woman. Or the very unlikely option that we might somehow become a threesome, a ménage à trois.

87

The steaming trunks and tea chests arrived from England, and we were excited to be unpacking them. All of our personal items and all of the things that we felt that we could not live without.

"Why did we bring this?" Christine was asking, waving some obscure kitchen utensil in the air.

"I have no idea at all," I had to admit.

Okay, so some of it was going to be useful, and some of it we could never replace. Like our wedding album, or the picture I had given Christine for her twenty-first birthday. But in reality, both of them disappeared into the back of the wardrobe never to see the light of day.

There was the set of dishes her parents had given us as a wedding present. We could hardly have it known that we had given them away, but we had been forced to buy a new set the moment we had our own place. The toaster, the kettle, they were easy, the electric supply was different, so they did not come. But Christine's wedding dress! The horrible burgundy thing that her parents had forced upon us because I was married before.

But almost everything found a home or hid quietly at the back of a cupboard, and there were a few treasures that we were glad to have with us again. Sometime soon we might even have some shelving to display these treasured trinkets, collected over the years.

There was a sale, and we stretched our finances to buy this half-price table and chairs. Not the most elegant things we had ever seen, but a balance between being functional, economic and not overly unattractive. Of course it was round, and our tablecloths were square, but life was a series of compromises for now.

We bought a futon bed. The put-you-up settee had proved so comfortable to sleep on, and the price was right. Now we no longer had the inconvenience of folding it down every night. We actually had a bedroom to use. Next month we would have bedside tables and a chest of drawers. The same store that had provided the futon had reasonably priced pine bedroom furniture.

Thus it was, we developed the habit of spending. Of course, we needed to furnish our new home, but it did become a habit. Our new television, a sound system, the stand to put this all on. Then in the kitchen, a microwave and a little toaster oven. By then we had done without so long ourselves that at last, it was time to treat ourselves.

Now we were earning reasonable money, we were paying the rent, feeding ourselves and looking forward to a brighter future. Where in England we would be lucky if we could afford to go out to eat three times a year, suddenly we could afford to eat out three times a month. Not at high-end restaurants but not fast food either.

88

"Sit down, someone will see you," Christine was mouthing up at me with a tense look on her face.

I looked back down at her with my 'what are you saying' expression.

"I guess that is the whole point," Christine said, and then relaxed a little.

A woman she had met through work, and who she had started to be friends with, had invited us to go to Wreck Beach. This was the local clothing optional beach, and as we would soon find out, it was a community in its own right. Despite the steep descent down some makeshift sandy stairs, it was a busy place.

There were food sellers who would lug their supplies in each morning and set up a make-do stand. There were salads and sandwiches made right there on the spot, and it was hardly worth bringing your own food and trying to keep it fresh. Then if things got slow at their stand, they'd carry a tray of their wares up and down the beach.

"Bagels, bagels, bagels," one of the regular vendors would call out as he approached, dressed only in a loincloth, with a convenient pocket in the front to hold his cash. There on his tray, freshly made bagels filled with salad.

There were drink sellers, "Ice cold drinks," was their call, as they approached with their coolers, and sure enough, you could buy cold pop all day. Yes, it was about three times as much as it would cost you in your supermarket, but oh, how welcome it could be on a long hot summer afternoon. People here did tend to make a day of it.

Fancy something a little stronger? A margarita perhaps, or pina colada, quite illegal but popular all the same. Young ladies would patrol the beach with their trays of frozen drinks, and not far away would be a young man with his cooler full of ice cold beer.

Yes, there would be police raids from time to time, and they would pour out the booze into the thirsty sand. There would be a stillness in the air until they left again, then vendors would head into the woods at the side of the beach where they kept their stash in well-shaded coolers. Very soon they would be back in business. It was an unwritten rule, no more than one police raid in any one weekend.

As we soon found out, you'd recognize the same people in the same spot on the beach, nearly every time you came down. There were families with the young children enjoying the sand, and most weekends there would be a face painter there to the delight of the kids. Sometimes someone would be making balloons into animals for them. But always a trained first-aider at one end of the beach, just in case of the occasional accident. She was a regular volunteer all summer long.

So I was totally happy to lay out naked and sunbathe or run down and cool off in the water. Christine declared that she was keeping her bikini bottoms on, but that didn't last very long. She soon felt herself to be more obvious partly covered than she would be fully nude. It was so refreshing to be able to relax and towel yourself dry after a swim without having to try to maintain your dignity.

We would spend a lot of summer afternoons enjoying the sun on this beach and knowing that we could be free to leave our things there with our towels while we took a swim because everyone would watch out for their neighbours' belongings even without any need to ask.

89

Other friends started to come into our lives, Martha and Eric, just before they broke up as a couple. That was fortuitous for me. Eric had tried to start some sort of photographic studio on the cheap. Full of enthusiasm, but without the financial backing, nor the business experience, it was never going to get off of the ground.

Now they were parting company and leaving their meagre flat on the Eastside, Eric had decided to give up on his photographic ideas, and while he had managed to sell a couple of his better pieces of equipment, he had a large boom arm on wheels that needed a little attention. Then to go with that, he had a mains-driven flash unit that no longer worked.

"Perhaps you can fix it," he said one day passing me a box of bits and pieces.

"Thank you, Eric, I will certainly try my best," I told him, excited by the possibilities.

Without a circuit diagram, it might be tricky, but I opened up the case one day to find a loose wire inside. A little solder and fingers crossed while I plugged it into the wall socket. Suddenly I had a mains-driven studio light. Okay, so it had this annoying habit of the modelling light going off and then ramping up from dim to bright before going off again. But the flash worked.

Now I had my two old rickety stands that had arrived from England, with my old battery-driven flash gun and mains-powered strobe with a couple of old beat up umbrellas. Plus a boom arm that was going to allow me to place a kick light high behind the model's head, just as soon as I could figure out how to attach any one of these lights to it.

It was all very basic, but I could make it work for me. I will be forever grateful to Eric for his donation to my photographic efforts. For getting me started again when there was so much else that we still needed on a more practical level. To top it all off, there in his box was a meter for measuring the strength of the flash. Not very accurate, but better than my previous efforts of measuring flash to subject distance with a tape measure.

Now what I needed was a model to photograph. Not always so easy to find, but Christine believed in my photography and was always interested in my favourite subject matter: attractive young ladies. She was always more successful at finding potential models than I was. It wouldn't be too long before I had an occasional photo shoot.

Christine was always on the lookout for models for me. She was my greatest resource. When I asked a girl if she would be interested in modelling for me, she would immediately and rightly take a defensive stance. When Christine asked a girl if she would be interested in modelling for her husband, that was a different story.

Of course, some of them were just not interested in modelling, and some of them were sure they were just not good enough, but some quickly said, "Sign me up, when can we start?"

90

It seemed that almost everywhere you went in the West End, every door to every shop or cafe would sport a little rainbow flag. Not only were gays welcome, but it was predominately gay. Restaurant tables were most likely filled with two guys dining together or two girls. The queue for the nightclub would be a long line of males, interspersed with a couple of girls, lost in each other's eyes.

Just very occasionally, you would see what was obviously the parents of one member of a gay couple, getting a guided tour of the West End. One of the few lucky enough to have come out, and been totally accepted by their family.

"It would kill my parents to even think that I had ever even looked at another woman," Christine would announce. Then she would seem to suffer a dark spell, almost as if she was worried that somehow word would get back to them. But for the most part, our new hometown was liberating for her.

We became quite used to eating in some of these local restaurants. No one took any more notice of a straight couple walking in through the door than they did a gay couple coming in. So if the food was good and the price was right, we would eat there.

It was so refreshing to be able to treat ourselves more often. It was that much less expensive to go out for a meal. Also, one big surprise was to suddenly find ourselves some weekends going out for breakfast. Hamburger Mary's was a short walk up the road, and besides all of the usual fry-ups, they did a delightful fruit salad with cottage cheese.

It was a great start to a sunny weekend in our new hometown. We were feeling more at home all of the time. Our apartment was coming together, and our shopping list was beginning to be more about things we wanted than it was about things we desperately needed. So we started looking out at our world with a wider perspective.

"Would you mind going in there with me one of these days?" Christine was asking as we were passing Little Sisters bookstore.

"Sure, no problem," I answered. "Do you want to go in now?"

"No, I am not ready," Christine said, hurrying on.

"Let's just have a look," I said, stopping in front of their window. "It is just a bookshop."

Little Sisters was a gay bookstore. They imported gay literature from around the English-speaking world, but mainly from the United States.

"There is no one here to be shocked or surprised to see us walking through that door, so let's just see what they have there," I prompted.

Once inside it was such a normal experience as we browsed the bookshelves, and this was the start of a whole new set of reading material for her. Half an hour later Christine walked out of the door with a copy of Babycakes by Armistead Maupin under her arm, discreetly placed inside of a plain brown paper bag, but it wouldn't be long before she would be sitting on the beach reading the rest of the series. She needed no more brown paper bags.

91

Little by little, we both became more relaxed around this new world we were living in. Wherever possible, I was there to support Christine as she tentatively explored her sexuality. But naturally, I couldn't be there for everything that she was doing for the first time.

She had discovered, in the pages of the Georgia Straight, the bi-focus support group, and she had summoned up her courage and contacted them. There was scant information about them, just enough to attract her attention and make her think that there might be something of benefit to her there.

They had agreed to meet with Christine over coffee, to tell her more and to vet her, checking that she was both suitable as well as safe to invite into the group. That was a Sunday afternoon, and I waited at home to see how she got on.

Suddenly the door opened, and without a word, Christine stomped in and threw herself down on the couch. I came around the corner to see her visibly shaken and angry.

"What happened; what's the problem?" I asked. "Were they nasty to you?"

"No, it's not them that I am mad about," Christine assured me. "They were great."

"Then what is it?" I queried.

"Three times I went to see those so-called sex therapists in England, three times. Damn them, no you are not gay, they told me. 'Oh, yes, don't worry, everything is fine; you are straight.'

Not once did one of them even hint that there was anything else." Christine took a deep breath and settled herself down.

Then she looked across at me and said, "I am bisexual. Ten minutes talking to these people and it was clear," Christine continued. "It is not so straightforward, that you are born one or the other. No wonder I am so darn confused most of the time. Why the hell couldn't one of these so-called professional psychologists tell me that there is such a thing as being bisexual?

"Damn that homophobic bitch that asked me in crude terms about groping another woman, and then dismissed me. They are supposed to be there to help and guide you. They are supposed to be sex experts. All they did was to set me back years."

"I am sorry," I reassured her. "I am sorry that we didn't know more ourselves, but how could we?"

"I want to strangle the lot of them," Christine continued. "They are getting paid good money, to sit there and play with people's lives. I may as well have asked advice from anybody I had passed walking down the street."

"It is hard to believe that these people can make their living like this," I told her, and I was flabbergasted too. "Are we somehow supposed to know this stuff?"

"Well, at least I am accepted into the group, and I am going along to their next meeting," Christine added. "I think that I have a lot to learn about myself from them."

92

'People watching', had always been a thing for us, and now more than ever, it was 'girl watching'. A nightclub in the basement of one of the local hotels became one of our early haunts. This one was straight, one of the few within an easy walking distance that was, but then it was mainly there for the out-of-town hotel guests.

We would order up a couple of stiff drinks and settle back to see who would wander in. Then in between girl spotting, we would get out on the floor and do some dancing. It was a relaxed sort of place, definitely not a hunting ground for the local wolves. Mainly visitors arriving in couples or small groups.

"Have you ever done any modelling?" Christine was asking our waitress one evening as she delivered our drink order.

"No," was all she replied. But she stood there waiting for more information.

"My husband here is a really good photographer, and we think you would make some really great photos."

"Can I think about that?" she asked.

We had been in there several times already, so we weren't total strangers to her. Our usual habit was to arrive early while it was still quiet, and there was plenty of room on the dance floor. We liked to have room to move. Once the floor was packed, you might as well sit down or just go home.

So it was Anna, the waitress, became my first photographic subject in Vancouver. Christine helped her relax, and she watched for things like labels sticking out or other unsightly distractions. I concentrated on the lighting and the camera.

This joint effort worked well, and I got some stunning pictures. It was refreshing to know that, at least, I could afford to buy a few rolls of film at a time, without trying to figure out what I would have to go without that week. Even though I didn't have the facilities yet to process my own films, I had moved forward a little with my lighting setup.

Some girls would feel more comfortable if they were just working one on one with me, but for the most part, having a girlfriend with them or just having Christine there would give them confidence. If we were lucky enough to be doing a second shoot, seeing previous results would work wonders.

But now I had a model scout, and she would prove far more successful at finding models than I ever did. It was a big help for my photography. Christine had excellent taste, a sense of what would actually work in pictures. Meanwhile, I was discovering just how big a part personality played in model photography. I had always just gone on looks, sometimes with disastrous results.

93

We were getting settled into our new life, enjoying ourselves and looking forward to all of the adventures to come. We could have lived in the moment forever, looking forward and never reflecting back on our not too distant past.

"I have been told today at work that I have almost two weeks of holiday to come to me," Christine announced arriving home from work one day.

"Lucky you," I said somewhat flippantly.

"I didn't think that I would get any this year," Christine added. "I thought that I would have to work the full year before I would qualify for anything, but apparently not. They told me that I need to think about when I am going to want to take them."

"Well, if they are telling you that you need to take them, then take them you must," I said, still being somewhat flippant.

"I guess so," Christine said in a matter of fact way.

"Well, you don't sound too excited about it," I looked across at her, not too sure what was going on for a moment.

"I don't want to go home," Christine declared.

"Oh." What else could I say?

"We promised my parents that I would come home for a visit as soon as I could," Christine was pensive. "When I couldn't go back as planned to pick up my papers, we told them I would do this the first chance I got. What was I thinking?"

"Well, then let's just get it out of the way while you have time off and I don't," I told her. "After this, we can get our holidays together, and then we can go off somewhere more interesting."

"I don't want to have to go at all," Christine stated.

I didn't fully understand why it was that she was so reluctant to go. But we had made a promise and gone back on it once through no fault of our own.

"Well, if we don't do this now we will forever have it hanging over our heads," I told her. "It is just the price of an airline ticket. I am sure that your parents will pick you up and run you around. I guess you won't get to do anything on your own, they'll have the whole two weeks organised long before you get there."

Christine sat there lost in thought.

"Let's check on flights and the price of a ticket," I suggested.

So, with that, the wheels were set in motion. We could have used the money in many other ways, but the ticket price was not too bad. The dates were worked out, and the letter sent, announcing Christine's plan. There was no way that her parents would say 'no we are busy, or away for that time period'. So, it was set.

I secretly wondered what mischief I could get up to while Christine was away, but in reality, I would work, come home, feed myself, watch some telly and head to bed. Just to do it all over again tomorrow and looking forward to Christine's return.

94

The time flew by, and soon I was meeting Christine at the airport. She was quiet and withdrawn, but it was a nine-and-a-half-hour flight. She would be jet-lagged and tired. It was only natural, it would take her several days to recover.

She just hugged me in the back seat of the taxi all of the way home. I was waiting to hear something about her visit, the highlights at least.

"I am so glad to be home again," Christine announced, as she threw open the door to our flat.

I trailed behind, pulling her suitcase.

Then she threw her arms around me and gave me another big hug.

"I am never going to do that again," she added. "I am never going to go home on my own, ever. If you are not there with me, then it is not going to happen."

"Well, you are not going to have to," I told her. "Besides, we have a lot of more interesting things to do with our holidays than to visit England."

So Christine told me briefly about her visit to her adopted grandmother, the highlight of the trip. A visit to a couple of other relatives, and of course the trip to Bath.

"Nothing has changed," Christine announced. "The same old people, following the same old routines. A cup of tea in the afternoon with that one biscuit each. Okay, you know what it is like."

"I do indeed," I replied.

"They are so far out in the country that a trip to town is a big deal. It is the highlight of the week, heck, month!"

Christine fell quiet for a while.

"You remember the kitchen table?" she asked. "Well, of course you do. We would sit there in the window for breakfast. Mum on one side, me on the other, and dad in the middle, and he would reach under the table and play with my knees.

"I had to try and stay away from him," Christine said almost to herself. "Even with Mum right there. I was standing talking to Mum while she washed the dishes, asking what was planned for the rest of the day. Then dad came up behind me and groped my bum."

I was totally lost for any response. I looked across to Christine and saw the beginning of tears in her eyes. I wanted to defend her. I wanted to make things right for her, but defend her from what? How could I make things right for her?

"Anyway it is over," Christine declared. "I don't want to talk about this anymore."

"You are home, and you are safe," I told her, "and next time, I will be right there with you."

And so her trip passed into history, and Christine gradually relaxed again, or at least for me, it disappeared from my mind. I had no way of knowing just how deeply this was burnt into Christine's psyche. Or how her childhood never quite left her alone.

95

"Are you here with anyone?" the guy at the next sink was asking me.

"Yes, I am here with my wife," I replied.

"Oh, pity," he added, walking back into the nightclub.

I headed back in myself, back to Christine, where I had left her standing at the side of the dance floor.

"I am not sure whether to be shocked or flattered," I told Christine. "I think this guy was trying to pick me up."

"That's what you get for coming into a gay club," Christine smiled.

Within an easy walking distance of our new home were several gay nightclubs, and while not all of them were places we would ever want to enter, this one had a wider range of clientele. Not everyone in the queue outside was gay or lesbian. Yes, it was predominantly gay, but then there would be gay couples with their straight friends. Or as in our case, couples in which one of them was discovering their sexuality, it was not as straightforward as it might have appeared.

So, once inside, the two things that mattered the most to us was whether there was a reasonable amount of room on the dance floor and whether the music was good to dance to. This club passed muster on both counts. The drinks were a reasonable price, and the people were friendly in nature if perhaps a little outlandish at times.

Some of the men would entertain themselves and the crowd by climbing onto the small ledges that surrounded the pillars supporting the balconies. They stayed there dancing the night away, or at least until their blood alcohol levels dropped and needed recharging.

Although there were not as many girls there on any given night, Christine did occasionally get asked to dance. I melted discreetly into the background, but Christine felt more confident knowing that I was just steps away. These weren't encounters that were likely to go anywhere, but they were baby steps in helping her feel more at ease.

Vancouver had other gay clubs that Christine would get to explore, both with me and without me, but it would take time for her comfort level to grow. But now she had her bi-focus group, and they would have occasional planned evenings out. Along with this, a few new friends appeared. They would drop by for coffee or invite Christine out to some event.

Dancing was something that we had always done together on the weekend. For years in England, we would often drive twenty-five miles to a decent nightclub, then twenty-five miles home again at two in the morning. It had been worth it. At one nightclub the whole ceiling was lowered down full of flashing, swirling lights, and the centre section turned over to reveal even more lights. Nothing as fancy here, but in other ways, it was more interesting.

96

"I got offered a job today." Bert looked across the work canteen table at me.

"You are going to take it, I hope," I replied.

"No, it is a government job, and it would mean moving my family every two years. I don't want to put my wife and kid through all of that."

"Bert, it's a secure, reasonably well-paid job, with a decent pension." I was somewhat surprised, and I added, "You do realise that this place is going bankrupt?"

"No," Bert looked a little taken aback at my statement. "We have just landed a forty-million-dollar order," he correctly pointed out.

"Yes, and we will never get to fill it," I told him. "Haven't you noticed how every time the delivery guy comes in to pick up a parcel that we are sending out, he waits for the cash?"

"But we have just moved into these bigger premises," Bert reminded me.

"Yes, it sounded good in the press report, didn't it?" I looked across at him. "Have you noticed all of the tours they are giving to well-dressed people in suits. They are possible investors."

"Yes," he sat waiting for more.

"We have a production line set up, and just before they are due to arrive, we start assembling our units. They arrive, we look busy, and then they leave. We then take the units apart again and sit around waiting for the next tour, because not only do the bosses not have the money to order more parts, they haven't paid for previous orders."

Bert looked a little pale. He wasn't sure that I was right, but he started to think about it. Two weeks later, we were laid off. The product was good, but the management hadn't been.

Now having at least some Canadian work experience on my resume, it didn't take too long for me to find my next job. This time as a technician, a little bit more money. Plus they had a bonus scheme. Every six months there was a payout. It looked pretty good on the surface.

I was testing power supplies. We left them working overnight and then ran a bunch of tests on them before releasing them to be shipped out to the customer.

One morning the boss came around. I was busy going along the line, testing my units. The technician on the next line wasn't doing much of anything.

"What is the big hold up here this morning?" the boss was asking. "These need to shipped out this afternoon," he declared.

"I am getting there," I told him. "They will be ready to go."

"Mine are ready to go now," Trevor announced, from the line next to mine.

"Good job," the boss congratulated him and walked away reassured.

"What?" I asked Trevor when the boss was out of earshot, knowing full well that he hadn't even started his testing.

"So?" Trevor said. "If any of them don't work when they get there, they will get a local techie in to fix them."

Then a few weeks later, Trevor was gone, and so was one other lad. I asked the lead hand about them, but he just shrugged his shoulders and walked off. They had not said a word about leaving to me, and I wondered what the story was. About six months later I found out. I hadn't qualified for the bonus cheque last time because I wasn't there long enough, but I should this time. The Friday before the payout date I was called into the office and fired.

They walked with me to my station and stood there while I collected my things, and then they escorted me out of the door. It was one hour before quitting time, and they expected me to quietly go home. I waited outside the gates and told the two new technicians what they could look forward to when it was time to pay out the bonuses.

But as it turned out they had done me a favour. Yes, I hated job hunting, and it wasn't easy in Vancouver. Though sometimes just being in the right place at the right time lets things work out in your favour. I happened upon a job fair, and although it didn't look very promising at the time, I was about to get a better job offer.

97

So, without even noticing it, I was entering some of the very best days of my life. Christine could never really leave her childhood behind, but I was totally unaware of that. She seemed happy, and we were close. Life was good. We were living in a beautiful place, the sea and mountains right on our doorstep.

Christine was finding models for me. Martha was just such a model from her bi-focus group. She was totally comfortable posing nude with some carefully placed flowers. I was getting some good pictures. Then she laid on our rug and Christine slowly decorated Martha's pubic hair area with freesias. With colour slide film in my camera, I shot down from directly above her. The cover picture of one of Christine's new books 'Secret Garden' had given us the idea.

Mary was about to teach me a valuable lesson. Christine brought perspective models along sight unseen, and I would do my best to create beautiful pictures for them. But Mary struck me as being somewhat plain. I wasn't going to tell her so, but I was wondering to myself, how am I going to get good pictures of her?

I was setting up my lights and getting my camera ready while they did the hair and makeup. "Just let me know when you are ready," Mary told me.

"Okay, I am ready; let's get some pictures," I said a little while later. With that Mary lit up like a Christmas tree. I was shooting colour slides, and it would be a week before I got the pictures back, but they would be great. Slowly the light went on in my head as I realised what it was: personality. Mary was able to project herself, project her personality into her pictures.

I would never have guessed it, but she ended up providing me with some of my very best portraits.

Another girl that Christine found who came to model for me was Emma. She was the cutest little thing, a pure delight, and we both flirted with her. One time we had run a bubble bath and poured Emma a glass of wine. I stood on the edge of the bathtub and shot down from above, and I shot pictures from the side. Then she stood in the tub and covered her body with bubbles. We had fun photographing her. We also started to become friends with her.

We both joined the local camera club, and I was soon winning awards with my pictures. I had been to a camera club back in England were everybody was always asking, "What sort of camera do you have?" Here, nobody cared what equipment you used, only how good your results were, what your pictures looked like, and perhaps the technical details of film and camera settings.

Bit by bit we became more involved in the club itself, taking roles on the executive board. Entering club competitions and displaying my pictures there within the club was good for my photography. Hearing critique from more experienced photographers, and answering questions from less experienced ones, also aided me in the development of my photography.

98

Elle was the driving force behind the camera club at that time; she was the glue that kept the club together. The Kingpin who got things done. I would always stand at the back of the room for club meetings, and whenever Elle started to ask, "Who would like to ----?" I swear hands were going up even before she had finished her question.

We went along to club outings sometimes. To the local bird sanctuary or on a fun scavenger hunt. Upon arrival, you were given a list of twenty subjects to find and photograph, all on one twenty-four exposure roll of film. Then we handed the film in, and the club would have it processed. A week or two later at a club night, you would see your results for the first time along with everybody else's, and the members would score your efforts.

The club and the club functions were good, but even more special to us were the new friends we were making and the invites. Elle invited us to her annual barbeque where we met an eclectic bunch of strangers, some of whom later became friends. It was a great evening out, after all of the food was consumed and a fair amount of the booze, her husband got his guitar out and started to play.

I discovered artists I had never heard of before but was soon to be a big fan of, such as Jimmy Buffet. Oh, how much I came to enjoy hearing his music, and Gordon Lightfoot's! I guess if they had made it over to England they weren't noticed, at least not within the music that I had listened to.

We were invited on boat trips, exploring the islands just off the Vancouver coast. A bicycling weekend on one of those islands where I was the slow coach. I would like to say that I was barely able to keep up, but it was worse than that. I couldn't even keep up going downhill.

But oh, the hot tub afterwards! One of life's great pleasures, I could easily have soaked there for hours. Give me a glass of wine in my hand, and some great company, and I was set. I was the first one in sometimes, but very often the last one out. So those were our summers.

My older half brother, who I had only ever met once before I left for England, announced that he was moving to the Okanagan. We were invited to share Christmas with them, and they made us feel as if we had always been a close family. We got to know my nieces and nephews that I knew of but had never met before. We now had even more family in British

Columbia, and somewhere new to visit in the summer too.

But while we were there, Christine mentioned cross country skiing. I don't know where that came from, but there was snow on the ground, and it looked like a winter wonderland. Perhaps Christine had seen their skis because she had never mentioned an interest in skiing to me before.

"You can try our skis," my sister-in-law offered.

"Sure," my brother had chimed in. "There is a flat area down by the river. We will take you down there in the morning."

I could barely manage to stay upright even while standing still, but that experience planted a seed. Not much more than a week later, that January Christine had found a course run by the local school board. Two hours of classroom training in what to wear and how to stay safe, then off to Manning Park to try the real thing. I still could barely stand up for more than a few minutes without ending up a heap on the ground.

But it was fun, and yes sure, I would be willing to try it again sometime. Well, the very next weekend we were invited out with a group to a local hill. The weekend after that we ended up getting a lesson in the hopes that it would help. Then we went to Mount Baker for a weekend ski trip, we skied every weekend for the rest of the season.

Then someone said, "You two should try downhill skiing." We did, and just like that, we were hooked. From then on skiing was a big part of our winters.

99

"There is this women's workshop coming up, and I would really like to attend," Christine announced.

"Okay," I replied.

"It is really expensive," Christine continued.

"How much?" I asked.

"Well, it is on the Island, and by the time I pay for the

course and my accommodation, food, and transport to get me there..." Christine was nervous about telling me.

"How much?" I asked again, as pleasantly as possible.

"I really think that it would do me good," Christine stated.

I just waited for the bottom line.

"It will be almost one thousand dollars," Christine blurted out, "but I really think I could benefit."

"It is my turn next time," I declared. I had my eyes on a set of studio lights to replace my old rickety stands.

"I can go?" Christine asked.

"Sure, when is it?

"Three weekends from now, so I will have to confirm right away." Christine still didn't sound sure that I was okay with this, but I was.

"Book your ticket," I told her. We were making reasonable money, but there was never much left over at the end of the month. There was always something to do, somewhere to go.

So off she went, and I had the weekend to myself. I would have loved to have some mischief to get up to. A little discreet something on the side, but I never did. It was just a fantasy that ran through my head sometimes. Christine had said that she didn't mind more than once while we were sharing our fantasies between the sheets, but in the cold light of day, it was different somehow.

So I stayed home and pottered about. I sorted out some of my slides. I thought about what I might enter next time at the camera club competition. I went to the local camera shop and daydreamed about some of the equipment they had there.

Sunday evening Christine returned, feeling bright and positive. "I am so glad I went," she told me. "And you will be too." She paused and looked straight at me. "I was thinking about leaving you, before the workshop, but all of that has changed!"

I had absolutely no idea, none at all. I was flabbergasted

and relieved all at the same time. I was speechless except to say, "Well then I am glad that you went." Then I just accepted that things had changed. I should have been asking questions. Not right then but in the days that followed. I should have made it my business to explore the issues, to ask why.

Things had changed, and I was the centre of attention in the time immediately following the workshop. The change was sudden with Christine's return from the workshop, but it petered out imperceptibly. Things returned to normal, and as I had always been happy with this, I took no notice.

"You guys are so good together," more than one of my models had said in passing comments. "You just seem to work in unison, but without having to talk about it."

"You two almost seem psychic in the kitchen, watching you work together," one of her friends had said. "My husband needs detailed instructions for every single move."

But in reality it was simple enough, we each got on and did whatever needed doing next.

100

Chrissy returned home from school to be greeted at the door by her father. Mr Wilson stopped her in her tracks. "The doctor came to see your mother today; she is very ill," he stated. "And we are going to have to look after ourselves for now. So go and change and then play very quietly." He added, "Perhaps it would be good if you played outside. Yes, take Brandy for a walk in the garden."

Chrissy did exactly as she was told. Uncertain what to make of this information. She was always glad to be out on her own, especially when she had her dog to talk to. "She must be sick Brandy if she wasn't there to scold me or ask about my homework. I am glad I don't have any to do, so I can just spend more time with you."

All too soon she was being called in, to a simple meal and a bit of television before her bedtime. "Come and quietly say goodnight to your mother," and her father led her as far as the door. There was no response from her mother, and she was led away again just as quickly. "Now get yourself ready for bed, I'll be in later."

Chrissy's father always came in to say goodnight. On a good day, he would pull the sheets up to her shoulders, kiss her on the forehead and be gone. On a bad night, well Chrissy didn't want to even think about that. Her mother was usually there expecting him back in front of the television. He would pop in while the adverts were on, or between programs.

Chrissy would always wait unable to relax until his good night visit was over. But she must have fallen asleep because suddenly she was awakened by him climbing into bed beside her. "Move on over, I am going to sleep in here with you, I don't want to disturb your mother while she is so sick."

Chrissy's heart began to race; she was trapped against the wall, unable to move, unwilling to move. He reached his arm over and pull her close up against his body. If I am perfectly still, she thought, and a tear rolled down her cheek. I must not sob, she scolded herself, and I must not let him hear me cry. Then frozen as immobile as she could make herself until at some point she fell asleep.

Morning time and Mr Wilson got himself out of bed and reaching down he ruffed up the bedding on the other single bed in the room. Just in case. Then for several days and nights more she wondered what it was that made her so bad that she made her father do these things. Her mind was calling out for help and praying that her mother would be well soon.

Finally, on the last morning of this new unwelcome routine, her father was up and out of the room. Chrissy put on her dressing gown and stepped through the door, out into the corridor. There was her mother standing across from her, just coming out of her own room.

Chrissy looked up at her mother's face, pleading for help, and with one quick step, her mother backhanded Chrissy across the side of her face. Landing a blow that knocked her sideways. "How dare you try to steal your father away from me!"

101

"I have a date on Saturday night," Christine announced. "Is that all right? We didn't have any plans did we?"

"No, that's fine. Do tell, who is she? Do tell, do I know her?" I asked a little surprised.

"No, I have only just met her," Christine added somewhat coyly. "I might stay over if things go well. Is that alright, are you sure you won't mind?"

"I will look forward to hearing about it on Sunday morning," I added with a smile.

This would be the first time that Christine had been courageous enough to go out on what she could call a date. I was excited for her and at the same time concerned that in finding herself I would lose her for good. I wondered how I would do being friends with a gay couple, one of whom had been my wife.

I had long expected that this might happen one of these days. Now I wondered how I would cope, after the shock of hearing Christine say that she had been thinking of leaving me. But then she had struggled with her sexuality for long enough so I would have to be happy for her when she found out who she truly is.

I thought of all these possibilities as I fell asleep that Saturday night, but I did sleep, and I awoke on Sunday morning interested to know how things had developed. But

Christine's expression as she came in through the door was not giving much away.

"Is that coffee still fresh?" she asked glancing across at the kitchen.

"It is good," I assured her, "I am only just on my second cup."

So she poured herself a cup and came and sat on the sofa.

"Well, how was it?" I asked. I had the feeling Christine was teasing me a little bit.

"It was fun; we had a good evening out. We drank a little too much and danced the evening away. She seemed quite taken with me." Christine allowed herself a brief smile.

"So, well?" I asked after a brief pause.

"Yes, we went back to her place to bed, okay I guess you would realise that as I wasn't here." Christine looked down at her hands. Then after a moment, "I had no trouble arousing and satisfying her, but she couldn't do the same for me."

Curious, I thought to myself, I had expected some answers from Christine's experience, and what I was left with is even more questions. What did this mean? I had no real idea, and I would have even less a few months later when her experience was the same with another girl. What was missing from this picture? I wasn't having the same trouble in our bedroom.

102

"Are you sure you don't mind?" I was asking Christine. "You are welcome to come along too."

"No, I am going to get myself ready for work tomorrow," Christine answered. "Have fun."

I was taking Emma down the road for a drink. The three of us had become friends, and when Emma was not here to model she would sometimes drop by or invite us over to her place. She'd even invite us to visit her at her workplace, which was an education for both Christine and myself.

Emma worked as a shooter waitress in one of the better stripper bars in town. She had no trouble lighting up the eyes of the young male customers as she approached with her tray of drinks, even though one of the girls might be undressing on stage.

"Are you ready for another round here boys?" she would ask a table of young men. Very often the money would come out along with a hefty tip, and the young men would compete for her attention until she moved on to the next table. Every round of drinks lessened her bill for her university education.

Christine and I would sit back away from the mayhem and watch the girls dance. Then as Emma emptied her tray of drinks, she would stop by our table for a visit. We would stick to our glass of beer or perhaps a glass of wine. Never one of her shooters. It was a fun evening out.

One evening we took her out to dinner in one of the better restaurants. It must have been mid-week because the place was quiet, just one other group occupying one other table. Our waiter was perfect, he held discretely back, but appeared as if on cue the moment we wanted anything. By the dessert course, Emma and Christine were openly flirting with each other. Feeding each other strawberries from their forks. I delighted in the whole process.

Just before we were ready to leave they took themselves off to the washroom, and just like that the waiter appeared with the bill.

"I hope that you don't mind me saying sir, but you are one very lucky man," the waiter offered.

"I am indeed, and no, I don't mind you saying so at all," I told him, and with that, I added a larger than usual tip to the bill.

Tonight it was my turn to flirt with her, at a pub just down the road, and after a couple of drinks, she walked me back home. Clinging to my arm, every step of the way. I was in my element.

103

I got an unexpected job interview from the jobs fair where I had dropped off my resume. I was escorted into an office on the fifth floor and sat one on one in front of this pleasant-looking gentleman. He started asking me questions about my electronics background. Not at all what I had been expecting. Humour him, I told myself, perhaps he is interested in electronics.

What does this have to do with standing there sorting mail for the Christmas rush? I didn't understand, but I answered his questions and tried to look interested.

"I would like to offer you a one-month contract," he said, and then he told me how much I'd be making.

'Yes please,' I was thinking to myself, it is more than I have ever made.

"Are you available to start on Monday?" he was asking me. "It would be on the day shift," he added. "We have two other people starting on the same contract, and they have taken the evening and the night shift so that just leaves the day shift."

"Oh that suits me just fine," I told him, and "yes I can start on Monday."

I had absolutely no idea what I was going to be doing, or what I had just let myself in for, but I needed the money. So it was something of a big surprise on Monday morning when I discovered a whole city block of sorting machines.

Then after a quick guided tour, I was presented with an industrial-sized vacuum cleaner and given a set of four machines to vacuum. So this is what my electronics training is all about, I thought to myself as I spent the next four weeks vacuuming the same four machines every day.

It was mindless work, but I could daydream. I could leave my body there doing the physical work while I imagined shooting pictures in a studio somewhere or walking along the beach or any number of other distractions.

The month passed quickly, and I had extra money to spend on Christmas. Then it was into the New Year, and I was back looking for a real job, without any luck at all. The phone rang, "Would you like to come back for a three-month contract?"

The money was good, and I didn't have any other prospects at the time. I went in and got reacquainted with my vacuum cleaner, except this time they started to teach me something about the machines and how to keep them running.

104

"Give me your engagement ring," I told Christine one evening.

"Yeah?" she questioned.

I held out my hand, and she peeled the ring from her finger. I couldn't believe that she had worn it all of these years and never once complained. I had promised to replace that lump of silver solder and that tiny chip of a diamond for our tenth wedding anniversary, but that hadn't happened. We just didn't have the money.

I had asked around and been told of this place in town, it's not a jewellery shop, but a place where they actually make jewellery, but only by appointment. I had already phoned in and booked to see someone the next day.

I arrived at the address to find an office block. Inside was the usual directory detailing the offices of lawyers and financial advisers and any number of different professionals. But I already knew that I needed the seventh floor, where I entered a little sitting area. There was a buzzer by a heavy-looking door, and I let them know I was there.

After being given the once-over through the glass panel, I was escorted past some workbenches into an office. It might have been any office anywhere, except for the large solid-looking safe against one wall.

The jeweller shook my hand and introduced himself before asking me, "What can I do for you today?"

I pulled the ring from my pocket and explained to him how I wanted to replace the mess in the middle with the nice looking diamond that really should have been there in the first place. Then I told him of my promise to upgrade it one day.

He took the ring from me and examined it. "Yes, I could do that for you. It looks as if it would be about point six of a carat. Let's have a look here." And he reached across to the safe and pulled out a long slim tray full of small brown envelopes, each one containing a single diamond.

He held a diamond close to the ring. "Something like this would look good in there," he told me, and he was right. It would be a huge improvement.

I waited for the bottom line, concerned about the cost.

"I could do this including the work for a little under eight hundred dollars," he said looking up at me.

"Oh," I told him. "You could be selling me a piece of glass for all I know about diamonds, but this is really special to me, and well, I was expecting to be spending a little bit more."

"Fair enough, I understand," he told me. Then he started looking through his collection of tiny envelopes. He pulled out a few more diamonds, one at a time, and held them up against the ring, dismissing each in turn.

"I tell you what I have got," he said pulling out yet another manilla envelope. "A beautiful Canadian diamond and it has just the right cut for a diamond solitaire. That would look great in there," he assured me while showing me the diamond.

"Okay," I told him with the hint of a question in my voice.

"I can do that diamond and all of the work involved in resetting the stone for twelve hundred dollars."

"Let's go with it," I told him, pleased with the likely results and yet still coming in within what I had set as my budget.

I left there with a light heart knowing I would finally be keeping a promise I had made so many years ago.

105

Christine had changed jobs too. A little more money, but a lot more job satisfaction. She had become the receptionist for a small group of psychologists, and they did their best to look after their staff.

Once a year sometime in late summer they took all of their staff, along with their significant others, out for a birthday dinner. At one time the staff birthday celebrations had been in the office with cake and some small gifts, but as the office had grown, that became less practical.

At Christmas time we all got invited to a fancy restaurant in a posh hotel. No gifts to buy or share, just a really nice meal at the expense of the management.

In the spring, they took all of us to a fundraiser. "Save our Souls" was raising money for a group of food runners. Every evening at closing time they had a team that would race around all of the local restaurants and collect up fresh but uneaten food. Then the next day, they would deliver a meal to people in need.

All of the local restaurants involved would be there, cooking a sample of one of their best meals for us to try. Then for good measure, the local wineries and breweries were there with sample size glasses that were being filled and handed out to us. Try a dish, move on, try another, sample some more wine and mix with a few other like-minded people.

Christine wasn't entirely happy being a receptionist at this point but it did help to feel appreciated. Though I had no idea that she somehow wanted a bigger challenge in her daily routine.

106

We went downhill skiing at Mount Baker that winter, and we stayed over in a hotel at the base of the mountain. There were a dozen of us, sharing dinner at the Chandelier restaurant and playing Pictionary in the evenings. The girls put on their swimsuits and climbed over a fence, breaking into the hot tub. It is a wonder we never got thrown out.

That summer we went off on someone's yacht and sailed around the islands. Six berths for ten people, but two slept on the deck, and two had their tent and went ashore to sleep. We had developed a great group of friends.

Plus we flirted with Emma. We took her to a concert to see Genesis. Going to a live concert was one of Christine and my favourite things to do. It was fun as always to go out as a threesome, and by this point, I think we both had a thing for Emma.

We had talked about what it would mean to become a threesome, and I definitely had some ideas of why it would be a good idea. But Christine asked, "Okay, how would that work?" And of course, I had no idea.

But Christine obviously wasn't totally against the idea. Sometime later Emma let us know that the house she had shared with several others was not working out. That she didn't know what she was going to do about finding somewhere she could afford. Christine cooked a really nice meal. She surpassed herself, and we used the evening to ask Emma if she would like to come and live with us.

Emma was sharp and never missed our intention, not for a second. She looked across at me and told me straight that I was too old for her, and she was right, of course. If it was just Christine, well maybe.

To her credit, we hadn't shaken nor surprised Emma. We

still enjoyed a great meal together and had our usual hugs as she left that evening. Happily, she soon found a new living arrangement, somewhat more conventional in nature.

107

After my three months as a temp, I was laid off right on cue. I did do some job hunting, but it was very difficult as there was nothing at the job centre. It's fix up your resume and go door to door, to the few odd electronics companies spread out across the lower mainland. But I had been assured by the union people that I would get a callback, and likely for a longer contract.

This time I was called back for a six-month contract, and I was being told that if I was to be there for six months and a day, I would become permanent, with all that entailed: medical and extended medical as well as getting into the pension scheme. I wasn't getting any younger, and I hadn't really worried about a pension, but perhaps it was time I did.

I needed this. Besides the benefits, I was earning ten dollars an hour more than I had anywhere else. Okay, the downside was that I didn't always get the weekends off and worse, I was alright for now, but when the shift bid came around, I would likely end up working the graveyard shift.

But if we were to have a solid future, this is what I needed to be doing, and long term, I knew I would get back to the day shift.

So I was on a term contract, and I was told to keep my 'nose clean' and 'get on with it'. Management did not like staff going sick, even though the full-timers had a certain number of sick days each year. If I did enough to impress, I might become permanent. Besides, I never liked to take sick days. It is like telling the universe, 'Hey it is okay, make me sick once and a while. I don't mind!'

It was a Saturday morning halfway through this six-month term. Of course, Christine was off for the weekend, but my alarm had just gone off, it was six-thirty.

"Call in sick," Christine suggested.

"I can't, you know how I feel about that," I told her.

"Go on, call in sick, I will make it worth your while." Christine looked up at me from the bed.

I couldn't help thinking that she wanted to make love, and then what about the rest of the day? But Christine was asking me to do this for her, so I went into the next room and phoned into work. Then I went back to bed. Looking back, I think that I must have been naive.

We made passionate love, and it was special. Then as I laid back on the pillow, Christine said "Stay right there; I am going to make us some breakfast." We ate in bed, and pushing our plates aside, we cuddled up. We dozed off for a while, but soon we woke and made love again.

"Come on let's make some lunch and bring it back to bed," Christine suggested. So we did. We made love twice more that afternoon in between naps, and then Christine put a frozen pie in the oven. We cuddled up tight while it was cooking.

We kissed and explored each other's bodies, and Christine somehow teased me into arousal twice more that evening before we fell asleep for the night. The next morning I got up and went to work. I should have been asking myself questions about what had just happened. But I was just pleasantly pleased with the idea that Christine was, at last, finding herself. That Christine was exploring and accepting her sexuality, whatever that turned out to be.

108

I had bragging rights at work. When one of our team complained about his wife expecting this, that or the other thing, I had an answer for them. When Barry complained that his wife was furious because he got caught looking at another woman, I told him if we are out somewhere and I happen to miss looking at an attractive woman my wife tugs my hand and points her out.

Peter was fighting with his wife because she thought that he should be ironing his own shirts.

"Why would you expect your wife to do your chores for you?" I asked.

"I don't know how to iron shirts," he complained.

"How old are you now, and you haven't learnt to iron a shirt yet?" He wasn't impressed.

Then Trevor was complaining because he had done his own chores, but his wife expected him to help with hers. "They are all household chores," I told him. "At home, we just get on and do whatever needs doing next until the chores are finished, and then we kick back and relax together. There is no such thing as Christine's chores or my chores, they are just household chores."

I wasn't always popular suggesting they might like to revisit their expectations.

Then I would take in some of my more successful and artistic photographs, I soon got used to who would appreciate them for what they were.

Finally, the six-month term was coming to an end, and unlike other terms, no one was reminding us that the term was about to expire. The union was telling us to just keep quiet about it. "Just show up on Monday morning for work as usual, if they don't turn you away at the door, you have a permanent job."

But the lad from one of the off shifts was worried about it. He couldn't contain himself. He marched into the office and told the boss that we should have had our notices by now.

"Just shut up and come into work on Monday as usual," he was told. With that, we became full-time staff.

It wasn't the most challenging of jobs, and it wasn't the

most satisfying, but the pay was good. There was extended health care, and I would soon be eligible to join the pension scheme.

109

Life was good. We had more money coming in, and we used it to the fullest. We moved within the same complex into a two bedroom apartment. I created a good darkroom for myself in the second bedroom. I started making large prints to enter into competitions at the camera club.

We bought ourselves a new computer. A forty megabyte hard drive. How would we ever fill that up? The Internet had not arrived yet, nor had emails, but I had had the chance to work on an early computer during my last electronics course. Then a friend had let me have the use of his while he was away. Now we had our own, and besides being able to update our resumes easily, we could also play solitaire and chess. Or maybe I was just a tech junkie.

We had bought ourselves a car, and it was better than anything I had ever expected to drive. Yes, there were monthly payments, but we could afford them. Then there were the insurance premiums that were higher than I had had to pay in England because they didn't recognise my safe driving record from over there.

Christine happened across a wardrobe makeover by a group that promised to make you look more professional at work. It was pricey, but it would boost her self-confidence, and she ended up with a bright new set of outfits. I reinforced her selection with positive feedback, even if I wasn't one hundred percent sure of all of her choices.

So we dined out, we danced at the local nightclub or went to clubs further afield. We went to see live shows. Phil Collins played here on his own and then again with Genesis.

We took a few romantic side trips or long weekend breaks over to Vancouver Island, or down into Washington State. Whitby Island was a delightful retreat, one of the oldest hotels on the West Coast, built in the style of a very large log cabin.

We spent time hanging out with friends. Or going to the camera club; by now I was writing for the club's monthly newsletter. But Christine started to lose interest in the club; in fact, she had lost interest in taking pictures all together. She had won some accolades in the beginners section, but without new work to enter it wasn't the same.

I would go on my own and bring back my little certificates showing that I had placed, with my pictures entered in the advanced section. Plus, I had work selected to send off to interclub competitions. I was doing well there.

But I started to notice that Christine was somewhat wrapped up in her own thoughts at times during the day. At night, as always, we held on to each other's bodies, even after all of these years, like two spoons in a drawer. Then on one boat trip, in particular, she seemed detached from the whole event, not just me.

110

Mrs Wilson was a stay at home housewife, looking after her family. She didn't have any choice. She didn't drive and had never been encouraged to learn. "You know with your one weak eye you would only be a hazard to yourself and other road users," she was told.

Her home was way out in the country, and the buses, well, they used to run through the village, but not anymore. "I will drive you in to get the shopping," was what Mr Wilson had told her. "No need for you to go on your own."

There was a library van that arrived every month, new reading material, and if she was lucky someone to chat to for a while. Then there was a grocery van that stopped by twice a week with fresh produce, but he never stopped for long, and so often these days, she was the only one that used it.

Mr Wilson participated in the local hunt. He helped to look after the hounds and spent time at the stables. He met up with people in his daily routine and had something of a social life, however limited.

So when summer arrived, and the house opened to the public, Mrs Wilson was more than glad of the chance to volunteer her services. Anything that needed doing even if it was only collecting tickets at the door. She had the chance to talk to people, to socialise, however briefly. She would busy herself helping out, getting involved, and there was always some time to chat.

"This is our special time together," her father would tell Chrissy, and he would take her to his tool shed and explain the function of each of his tools. Chrissy got to handle them and started to see how each might work. It fascinated her and developed her curiosity. There was the potting shed, with tender young plants just beginning to push there way up through the soil. Chrissy was encouraged to help, then even to have some of her own plants, and later her own patch in the vegetable garden.

But the petting and the cuddles filled her with dread, and she couldn't understand what it was about her that made her father do these things. She was confused and trapped. She loved her parents, and they were good parents, so how could she be so bad? She didn't know what it was that she was doing wrong. However, her mother let her know in no uncertain terms that she was somehow to blame.

"What do you think you were doing, you little trollop?" her mum was asking as she struck Chrissy across the tops of her legs with a riding crop. "Don't think that I didn't see what you were up to in the greenhouse. Don't you dare," her mother fumed as she brought the crop down hard one more time.

Chrissy looked forward to the time when she would be old enough to leave home. She daydreamed and tried to imagine what it would be like. She fantasised about a time when she wouldn't have to be the subject of her father's unwanted affections anymore.

111

Christine had picked up the mail on her way home from work, and she sat there reading an airmail envelope which could only have come from her parents. As she finished reading, she gripped it with a clenched fist, then dropped both fist and letter into her lap.

"What's in the letter?" I asked, somewhat concerned. She usually finished these occasional letters with the statement, 'same old, same old'.

"It is coming up to my father's sixty-fifth birthday, and they are planning a celebration."

"They're expecting us to be there?" I asked.

"Something like that," she said. "I don't want to go. If we are spending that sort of money, I want to be going on holiday somewhere nice," she added.

"Well, we could blend it in with a holiday of our own, and just be there for the party," I offered.

"I don't want to be holidaying in England," she stated.

"Instead of flying into London, we could fly to Paris and then just catch the ferry across for the birthday party, then back to Paris to finish our holiday." I left that idea hanging out there in the air.

"I don't want to go at all," Christine closed the conversation for now, but it was something that we would have to think about and talk about some more.

It had been many years now since Christine had had to deal with her parents at all. The occasional letter, Christmas cards and birthday cards, that was about it. Apart from that, they had been put out of our minds for the most part.

I was very aware of how she had felt on her previous return from her solo trip, but I would be there this time. I wouldn't be leaving her alone at her parents' place. But how could you say no to such a milestone birthday? All I could do was to offer my support. Well, it wasn't my decision to make.

They had given us lots of notice, in the hope that we would be able to arrange to be there. They knew that we would both have to fight to get the time off, but it was later in the year, well after the summer holidays were over. So we should stand a good chance of both getting the same two weeks.

I had already had to bid for my holidays, and now I would have to try to change them. But I had also been required to bid for which shift I wanted to be on, by seniority. I knew that I would have to leave the day shift. That being said, I would in all likelihood end up on the graveyard shift. There was less staff on that shift, so with luck, more chance of getting the weeks that I would want.

112

"I am doing this for us," I stated. "I don't want to be away from you at night, but I need this job, and we need the money." I had just been told that I was going to the graveyard shift.

Christine slumped down into a chair, trying to find some way to fend off the inevitable.

"You know that there is nothing in this province that is going to pay me the same sort of money, except perhaps a logging camp, and then I would be away from home for weeks at a time."

"I know," Christine offered in a meek voice.

"In just one more year, I will be able to get into the pension scheme, and we will be glad of that down the road," I told her. "We already have extended health care, we might not need it right now, but it is there." I was trying to reassure myself as much as I was Christine.

"We will have all sorts of benefits down the road," I continued. "I already know that I am going to need glasses one of these days, and then there is your favourite," I paused for effect, "dental coverage."

"Oh, yippee," Christine tried to manage some humour.

Christine had real trouble getting herself to go to a dentist. It took a major toothache and a lot of denials before she would go. Even then it required something to calm her nerves and a general anaesthetic to keep her in the chair.

I felt for her. It had taken nearly as much to get me on that aeroplane. But you had to go, there really isn't any choice, and putting it off just made matters worse.

So there we were looking at me going to the night shift, which was eleven-thirty at night until seven thirty the next morning. We would be passing in the doorway as I got home and Christine left for work. In the eleven years of our married life, almost every night we had been wrapped up in each other's arms.

Yes, we had had a small taste of what this would mean years ago in Christine's time as a nurse when she had to work the night shift, and again five years ago when she went home to her parents. It was going to be hard on both of us. This meant five nights a week!

But then we would have the evenings together. We could still go out to a show, the movies, or invite people over. Yes, it would be a challenge for me to get my body clock back to days, but I would have two days off for my weekend.

I would have taken a pay cut, I would have done just about anything to have stayed on days, but I was trapped. I needed this job and everything that it would mean for our futures.

Slowly it dawned on me that it was going to be even harder than I had first thought. Yes, I had to work some weekends on the day shift, and I would likely still have weekends to work on night shift sometimes. Then Christine would be home on her weekends off, wanting to get on and do things, and I would be trying to sleep.

There would be offers of boat trips or weekend ski trips, but I couldn't control when I would be working. Would Christine want to be heading off with our friends? I could hardly hold her back just because I couldn't make it.

113

"You did tell me that I could get to see a psychologist on your extended health care?" Christine asked some time later.

"Yes, you can get up to ten appointments a year; are you thinking of seeing someone?" I asked.

"Can you help me find somebody?" Christine asked

"Sure, we can do some research, but you should pick someone out yourself," I offered.

"I just don't know where to start, so if you can help that would be great," Christine added.

She was a little sheepish about the whole thing, but who could blame her. She'd had nothing but bad luck in her attempts to get help before, and that had stopped her from reaching out for help. But Vancouver seemed a more open-minded society so I couldn't imagine that she would meet a homophobic counsellor here.

I was excited for her. She was finally feeling able to face her past and get some help. Yes, she might very well discover that she was indeed gay and that somewhere down the road, I would have to face her moving on. But this could mean the world to us if she could face her past head-on and exit out the other side.

So we did a search, and she found someone within easy walking distance, and as she quite rightly said, "Until I see him, I am not going to know whether I will be comfortable talking to him. Or indeed whether he will be able to help me at all."

So as it turned out, it was possible to get an early evening appointment on her way home from work. There was a small user fee that she would have to pay herself each time, but the rest would be charged directly to my extended health care.

An appointment was made, and I had high hopes for her. Hopes that this would be someone that could actually help her. Hopes that she would feel free to talk openly to him about all of the problems that she faced. I waited at home, feeling optimistic as she returned from that first visit.

"How was it?" I asked as she walked through the door.

"Okay," was her reply.

"Did you feel comfortable talking to him?" I added. I was full of questions, but I wasn't about to get much in the way of answers.

"I think so; we'll see. I have another appointment next week," Christine added, and that was it for now.

One week later Christine was there again, and I was awake and waiting for her when she got home. I was still optimistic if somewhat puzzled by the lack of detail that she offered on her return. But it was early in the sessions. This whole process was going to be difficult for her. I could truly appreciate that.

"He would like to see the two of us together," Christine stated. "Would you be willing to come along with me next week?" Christine asked.

"Yes, of course, I will," I offered, and that was the end of the subject for now.

114

The following week I had set my alarm so that I would have time to get up and be showered and dressed, and down to the psychologist's office for our appointment. It wasn't far at all, and I walked briskly to make sure I was there in good time.

It was just another downtown highrise. Nothing to distinguish it from any of the other buildings in the area and nothing to make it obvious just who it was you were visiting in the complex of offices.

I announced my arrival to the receptionist and was told to take a seat. A small waiting area with a few chairs, a coffee table and of course the usual collection of magazines. As I sat there, I assumed that I was waiting for Christine to arrive.

But as I was watching the outside door, it was the inner office door that opened and out stepped a very presentable middle-aged man. He greeted me by name, and as I arose, we shook hands.

"Come on into my office," he said, then with a sweep of his hand, he led me to the door.

I was totally surprised to find that Christine was already there, seated in his office, and I would have naturally headed to the chair beside her, but I was pointed to the lone chair opposite the other two. It was a somewhat uncomfortable and strangely unexpected situation.

"We have asked you to come along today because Christine has something that she wants to tell you," the psychologist announced.

I was puzzled and uneasy; this was all so much different than what I was expecting.

"Over to you Christine," he continued.

Christine looked at me and then hung her head. She went to speak, but nothing came out. She gathered herself and tried again.

"I am leaving you," Christine told me, her voiced cracked and a tear rolled down her face.

I was totally unprepared for this. I felt a shock wave move through my body.

"But why," I asked.

"I can't tell you; I love you so much." And now tears rolled freely down Christine's face.

What am I supposed to do; what am I supposed to say, I'm asking myself. How am I to deal with this? I am not to know why, just that she is leaving me.

How long had it been? Just a matter of weeks ago, when Christine had told me, "I could never leave you." Now, this, and friends were telling us, "You guys are so good together." They were right, now what?

I was in shock, bits of information were being expressed. But I couldn't take them all in. I was looking at Christine, and she was barely holding herself together.

"I can't expect you to wait for me," she was saying. Then she continued to empty the box of tissues she had held on her lap.

I had no way of processing what little information I was getting, and no way of making sense of any of it. I couldn't have seen this coming, and now our time was just about up.

"Why don't you go on out and make yourself an appointment for next week," the psychologist was saying to Christine. Quickly she was up and out of the door.

Then he turned to me. "What do you think Christine meant by that, telling you that she can't expect you to wait for her?"

"I don't know, I supposed that she would not expect me to wait," I ventured, not knowing where this was going.

"Okay, but I think she is hoping that you will wait for her," the psychologist was telling me. "I can't tell you what is likely to happen," he added, "but she thinks so much of you, I wouldn't be surprised that if you give her time, this will all be sorted out."

"Now I would like to see you on your own if you could

manage that. Don't bother right now but do phone in and make an appointment," he said passing me his business card.

We walked home in silence. What could I say? I was just about holding myself together.

"I am sorry," Christine muttered. She was still shaking and still had tears in her eyes.

115

Somehow we managed to throw together some dinner. Neither of us had managed to say very much at all. We washed our dishes and danced around each other carefully and thoughtfully. Not wanting to rock the boat or step on each other's toes, and generally not knowing how to proceed.

"So how and when is this going to happen?" I asked.

"I am not sure yet," Christine told me. "I have found an apartment up the road, and I have my application in, just waiting to hear."

"I won't be very far away," she offered as if that was going to make this easier for me.

I sat there dumb for the moment; my whole world had been shaken to its very core.

"We will have to go through our stuff sometime and sort things out." Christine continued. "I am going to need to take enough with me to get me started."

"Take what you need," I told her. "Stuff can be replaced."

We were being as careful with each other as we could be. Trying not to say or do anything that would make the situation any worse. Christine was feeling a sense of relief, having found the courage to tell me. It was out in the open. That was her biggest hurdle.

For my part, my mind was racing, just trying to make sense of this. Trying to put an optimistic spin on this revelation. Maybe a whole new relationship was out there waiting for me.

Maybe I could get out there and have some fun, play the field.

Yes, this could be good for me too, a new start. I was trying hard to be positive. One door closes, and another one opens. Just don't think about the facts. Don't let yourself dwell on the fact that the fifteenth anniversary of our first date was just two weeks away.

Christine won't remember that, nor will she be thinking two months from now about our twelfth wedding anniversary. I must not be thinking about these things either. Just hold it all in, I told myself, you will get through this.

Somehow the world didn't stop turning, and we got through the evening. I was grateful that I didn't have to face going to work. I had a couple of days to adjust, to compose myself, as I started to wonder, how is this going to work?

It is likely going to take a month, living together, or rather sharing this space. How will that work, because now it was bedtime. We had always slept in close physical contact. What if I forget in my sleep, and reach out to hold her?

Christine went in first, and I dragged my feet in the bathroom, not sure what I was about to face. When I went in, Christine was in bed, and I climbed in beside her, feeling awkward. I was searching for something to say.

"I know that it is a lot to ask," Christine broke the silence, "but would you mind holding me?"

116

"Would it be all right if I take the television with me?" Christine was asking a few days later.

"Sure, of course," I told her. "Take whatever you need."

"Thank you," she continued. "You can keep the music; you really enjoy listening to your music."

"Yes, but you do, too," I replied. "Besides half of this music is yours. You need to go through it all and take your albums."

"Okay, I will take some of the music that means the most to me. I will have to pick up a cheap player sometime."

"Take what you need," I said. "If you need the player, take it, I will sort something out for myself."

"No, you are going to need your music," she told me. "I will sort through the records and show you what I have picked out if that is okay."

The silences were untenable. We had never had a situation where we had to tiptoe around each other's feelings. Not once since our engagement could I remember a situation where we were not moving forward together.

"I guess I had better take the set of dishes that my parents gave us as a wedding present," Christine said.

"Yes, it would not do for them to ever learn that you had let them go." I knew that she would rather take the new set that we had bought ourselves. "We can split the cutlery, as there are eight pieces of each after all," I added.

We continued to be more than generous with each other, and I really didn't mind what she took with her. She was the only thing that I really wanted to keep. Everything else was just stuff.

But we found the one thing that we both wanted to have. As a child still in school, Christine had taken pottery classes, and she had made this beautiful china lamp base. It was elegant and far more delightful of an object than you would expect from a school class. It was a little part of her.

"If I ever tire of it I will return it to you, I promise," I told her, and so I became the custodian of a small part of Christine's history.

"Will you help me move?" Christine was asking. "At the end of the month, I hope to get the keys on the thirty-first."

"Yes, I will help you move." It was the very last thing that I wanted to do, and I would be told a dozen times what a fool I was. Friends suggested, "Let her get on and move; come on this boat trip with us." But as much as I didn't want to be moving her out, I didn't want some strange male face arriving to pick up her things.

117

So I made my own appointment to see Mr Peterson, Christine's psychologist. I desperately needed to talk, and especially I needed to talk to someone who wouldn't be trying to lay blame on Christine, someone who wasn't dismissive of my pain and confusion.

My brother explained to me how women were like buses, and that there would be another three along any minute now. I could have throttled him, but I knew that he would be just as devastated if the shoe were on the other foot. He was there for me, yes, a five-hour drive away, but he was there, and I would be glad of his support.

My best friend at the time listened intently and didn't try to apportion blame, but he tried to assure me that six months from now I would be over it, and ready to move on. But I knew that hadn't been true for him. I was sure it wouldn't be true for me either.

In work, oh how I wished I hadn't bragged about how good a relationship could be. Often I was asked, "So what were you arguing about? Really, you must have been fighting about something. That is ridiculous; people don't just leave for no reason at all! You must have done something. What did she tell you? It doesn't make any sense."

"No, it doesn't make any sense to me either," was all that I could reply.

Luckily, some of my female co-workers were more understanding and more ready to just listen, because I was replaying all of this over and over in my mind. I was just trying to find something to hold on to, in my circling confusion. Just trying to find something to make some sense of it all.

Oh, but Mr Peterson, he is a professional. He is sure to help me cope, and I had asked him straight out, "Is it professional to be dealing with both of us at the same time?"

"Yes, that is not a problem," he reassured me. "Of course, I can't tell you anything that Christine is saying to me, nor her of you. But yes, I can deal with the two of you separately."

So I sat, and I talked to him, I poured my heart out. I told him how difficult it had been for Christine over the years, trying to face and deal with the abuse she had suffered. I talked at length, about how it had shaped our relationship at times, and how I really hoped that she could finally face it, deal with it, and come out the other side a stronger person. I told him how although this was painful I was excited for her, as finally she was feeling strong enough to face her past.

But then he floored me. He shook me to the core. He took what little I thought I knew about what was going on and he trashed it.

"I'm sorry, but the abuse she suffered is your issue to deal with, that is not what she is talking to me about," he told me as our session was drawing to a close.

118

Some evenings I could almost imagine that this wasn't happening. We would share a nice meal, we would wash up and tidy up, then sit on the sofa together watching our regular programs. We might talk a little about our day, and if one just looked at the moment, it looked as if everything was fine.

We would go to bed and sleep wrapped up in each other's arms, and it felt so normal and natural. Yes, Christine had told me that she didn't want to have sex with me anymore, but if I lived in the moment and didn't think about what was happening, the pain would subside.

But then there were times when a conversation would start. I really needed to make some sense of everything. I had been told that this was not my fault, that I had not done anything wrong. So why? Why was this happening? I had been told that there wasn't anyone else. I had imagined that Christine was ready to deal with her past, but this doesn't seem to be the case.

I had pried gently in trying to understand what it was that was happening, to us, to Christine, to me. But I got no feedback at all. Nothing to help me make sense of anything. Then as if it wasn't painful enough, as if it wasn't hard enough for me to cope, one night Christine announced, "I just need somebody that is going to be there for me."

That was a real slap in the face. "I am there for you," I replied. "I have always been there for you."

"I know," Christine admitted. "I'm sorry."

I had to turn away, to hide the tears in my eyes.

Somehow we got through the month; a month that I hoped would never end, but end it must. Christine had her application accepted, and she was told that she could get the keys on the thirty-first, and so I was geared up to help her move.

It wasn't far, and most of the things she was taking were not too big. Our apartment had become little piles of stuff. Collections of things that were hers or mine, and then suitcases filled with clothes. There was disruption everywhere. I was trying to be strong for both of us.

119

Moving day arrived, and we were left waiting for the first few hours as Christine didn't have the keys yet. A phone call, a wait, another phone call. Finally, we were underway. Just the two of us, carting and carrying Christine's things the two and a half blocks to her new home.

I was hot, tired and covered in sweat. Far too busy to stop and think or feel depressed over what it was we were doing. But at last, everything was there, including our cat. Christine had decided that she wanted to take Merlin with her, into her new life.

"Have you thought about what you are going to want to eat for dinner?" I asked Christine.

"No, it hasn't even crossed my mind," she admitted.

"Okay, here is what I am going to do," I told her. "I will go home and shower and change, then I will pick up some chicken and fries up the road here, so we can eat!"

"Oh, that would be great," she said, somewhat relieved.

"Then after we have eaten I will help you get things set up and ready for use," I offered.

"Thank you so much," Christine was glad not to be left with this pile of pieces of shelving as well as the cables for the television to sort out.

So less than an hour later, we were sat eating out of styrofoam dishes with plastic forks. It tasted divine after all of the work we had put in that afternoon, and I had even thought to pick up some cheesecake for a little dessert!

We assembled the shelving, connected the television and got it working. Then we moved boxes and made sure that Christine was organised and had everything she would need to start her new life.

We were finished in time for the fireworks display. Each of the evenings of the fireworks we had walked down together to the beach and watched, as we could not see them from our apartment. But now I walked out onto Christine's balcony, reached out and held the railing. We wouldn't be able to see the lower fireworks, but everything in the air, we would ha an unobstructed view.

"They are just about ready to start," I warned Christine.

"I am here," she stated, stepping out onto the balcony.

Then she stepped in front of me and backed up into my arm. There we stood, me with my arm wrapped around her, watching the fireworks, just as we always had. To anyone watching from another balcony, we would appear to be a close, affectionate couple, enjoying an evening together.

"You should write my book some day," Christine said out of the blue, without even turning to look at me, and with that the first fireworks lit up the evening sky.

When the fireworks were over, there was nothing left for me to do than say goodnight and head for home. It was sheepish and awkward, I had no idea what to say as Christine opened her door to let me out.

I stood and faced her. She threw her arms around my neck and started to sob. Finally, she let go, and I stepped back, still facing her.

"I love you so much," she said.

I just turned and walked away. I heard the door close quietly behind me.

120

I lay on my back staring blankly into space. I was in too much shock to feel anything. I didn't cry; I just lay there. Somewhere in the night, I rolled over in my big empty bed and hugged bedding. I slept and accepted that sleep was to become my only escape for quite a while to come.

In the morning I couldn't get out of there fast enough. I have somewhere to go. I drove the five hours to ace, trying to just concentrate on the road. I was ink of anything else, especially to not remember ne I made this trip was with Christine right

The tears welled up in my eyes from time to time, but I managed to choke them back down to keep my concentration. I knew that my brother was not going to know what to say or do, but it would be a safe place to spend those first few days. My sister-in-law would listen. She wasn't about to judge or tell me to go back and do this or that, she just listened.

Anytime I felt the need I would disappear into my room or slip out the back door into the garden. I didn't have much of an appetite, but I needed to eat, and the food was there without my having to think about it. The family never drank very much, so there was no temptation to use that escape route.

The sheer shock of it all was starting to wear off, I started to break down and cry when alone sitting in the bedroom with my head in my hands. This is not a good place for this, I realised. The family is not going to know how to cope with me if I really do just lose it.

Yet I was so glad not to have had to spend those first few days on my own. Even if I felt that I would sometimes have to help them cope with me. I made it over the first hurdle. Thank goodness it was a long weekend and that I had those few days off.

It was time to take the drive home and to face that big empty apartment on my own. Somehow I did it. I concentrated on the road. I was extra careful amid so much traffic.

It was a long drive, yet part of me hoped that it would never end. Just the car and me and the road sliding by. I wanted nothing to deal with, and nothing to think about or handle. But I did arrive home, and I dragged myself out of the car and up to my empty place.

As I swung open the door, there was Merlin's meow to greet me. "Christine," I called out. There was no answer. My heart had soared for a moment, then come crashing down again just as fast. There on the table was a note.

It read, 'Merlin cried all night that first night and in

day. I couldn't handle it anymore, so I brought her back to you.'

I made a fuss of Merlin. I had no idea how it was that she had become my cat. We had adopted her together, and we had both looked after her. I hadn't noticed her having a leaning towards me more than Christine. But Merlin was home now, and she settled right back in. There were times I would be glad of her company.

121

Work was extremely difficult. I hadn't been on nights long enough to really get to know many of the people on the shift. I hadn't had the time to get into a routine of sleeping during the day. Soon the shock of losing Christine had just become the pain of losing Christine.

It wasn't always busy, and when the machines were working as they should, we were just covering the floor, waiting for the next incident. My situation would suddenly hit me, and I would break down, quickly scurrying to hide between machines or disappearing into the washrooms. I would vanish into the storeroom as if looking for some part or other, just to have somewhere private to cry.

I was very aware that Christine was in her new home or somewhere fast asleep. I would watch the clock, not to know how much of my shift was left, but to wonder if she was sleeping. Then first thing in the morning I would often suddenly become aware of her as if she had just woken up somewhere.

It seems unlikely to me now, but some days even if I was 1e middle of fixing a broken down machine, I ' become aware of Christine. A quick glance l I would know that it was time for her to be t ready for work.

ite to talk to anyone who was willing to listen.

I was talking this over in my head all of the time, trying to make some sense of it all. Just looking for any small ray of hope. Trying to understand what was happening to us and why. Trying to understand that if there was some sort of problem as there must be, why couldn't I be told about it.

Could this really be so drastic that we couldn't talk this out? Make some changes? Do things a little differently? Solve this mystery? So although I continued to see the psychologist he was of little help other than being someone that would sit and listen, and oh how fast an hour would fly by when I had so much in my head.

I made it clear to him how confused about this whole event I was, and how much pain I was in. It had quickly become impossible to hide my broken heart from the world. Even though I had tried to carry on as normally as possible, everyone who knew me would instantly realise that something was not right.

The camera club had always been a source of interest and inspiration, but now it was just somewhere to be. I was so obviously down, and I found myself trying to explain my situation again and again. A situation that I didn't even begin to understand myself.

122

I had not seen much of Christine at all. Perhaps once or twice we had met up on the corner of the road when I had some mail that had arrived for her. Oh, I wanted to see her so badly, but what could I say, and twice a day on my way to and from work I would look down her street, and up to her balcony to glance at her bicycle hanging out there in space.

Then I had a call asking if we could meet up, but the tone of her voice gave me no hope that it would be for anything positive or in my favour. But, as arranged, I waited for her outside of my apartment building. She looked subdued and barely glanced up at me as we met.

"I don't want to come inside," she stated. "Can we just walk down to the beach and talk?"

"Yes sure," I told her, feeling uncomfortable and unsure as to what this was all about.

But we just made small talk as we walked along until we were down at the sandy beach, and Christine was looking around for somewhere with a little privacy.

"Let's sit over here on this log," she suggested.

The summer season was over, and although it was a pleasant evening, there were not too many people around. So we sat on the log, facing each other, and Christine looked up at me. Very briefly looking into my face and then she looked down again.

She was hesitant to start, but then, at last, she said, "This really is over. You are going to have to let go and move on."

I felt the tears welling up in my eyes, and I didn't know what to say, as I didn't know where this was coming from.

"I am sorry that I have hurt you," Christine continued. "But this is for the best; this is what I have to do."

I sat looking at her, unable to respond, with tears rolling freely down my face.

"You must have seen this coming," she was telling me, and I was shaking my head, no. "I have moved on," she was adding. "Now you need to do the same thing."

I just lost all control and any self-respect, and I just sobbed openly. I was shaking, crying, the tears rolling down my face, and I could not stop.

Christine leant forward and put her arms around my neck, and I cried. I held onto her, I shook uncontrollably and wept openly, totally unaware of anything else except this incredible loss. Where had all of my hope and optimism gone? What had happened to Mr Peterson telling me that he thought that she had hoped that I would wait for her?

I was well beyond wondering what had brought on this unwelcome meeting. Why had Christine felt the need to rub this in so hard? Where was this coming from? I was way past anything but pain, and I hurt like I had never hurt in my life before.

When finally the tears had stopped, and I had regained some of my composure, we got up and walked back up the beach, and on up the hill towards Christine's place, avoiding walking in front of the building we used to call home.

We arrived outside of her new apartment complex, and I was going to have to say goodbye, but this time with no hope of ever even holding her again. With that thought, the tears were returning to my eyes, as we held hands and looked at each other.

Then she asked me, "How would you like to date your wife?"

"I would love to date my wife," I told her, and I walked off with at least a little glimmer of hope in my heart.

123

So I waited with that little ray of hope, but I heard no more about going out together. Twice a day I looked up towards her apartment, just to glance at that bike, with the front wheel hanging over her railing. On my way to work each evening and on my way home in the morning, but that was all I saw.

I sat and talked to the psychologist. I poured my heart out and was trying to make sense of it all. Trying to find something to hang on to. But Mr Peterson let me talk without giving me anything new, nor any hope.

Until near the end of our session, he then asked me, "Do you love your wife?"

"Yes, I do," a little surprised by his question.

"I mean, do you really love her?" he asked again. "How much do you love her?"

"I love her unconditionally," I told him.

"Then I am going to ask you to make me a promise," he paused, and I waited for more.

"I ask you to promise me right now that you will let Christine go and never be the one to initiate contact. I am worried about her," he continued. "I am worried that if you put any pressure on her at all, she might do something serious. Something we would both regret."

"Can you promise me that?" he asked again.

"I promise I will never be the one to initiate contact," I told him, and I was left to worry about what Christine was going through. Forced to step away, and perhaps never to know how she was doing.

Work was hell, being home alone was even worse. But then if the phone were to ring, I would be there to answer it. However, the hours could become long and tedious, and I would crave company.

There were few choices for me. I didn't want to be out anywhere that Christine was likely to be, and I didn't want to be out somewhere retracing our steps. I didn't want to think that the last time I ate here, it was with Christine, or the last time I danced with her was here, that would be even worse.

There was a pub in town we had never gone to, but where a friend's son worked as a bartender. If I arrived in the early evening, he would recognise me and stop by to chat between serving costumers.

He knew only that we were apart, and it was too public a place for me to want to share any details, but it was also the only place in town where someone would recognise me and say hello. So I would stretch my evening out over two pints of beer, then walk home hurting more than I might have had I stayed in.

124

It had been six weeks since Christine left, and I hadn't heard any more since that dreadful night on the beach. But I believed in us; I believed in our relationship. I understood that Christine had things in her past that she had never dealt with, and I had thought that was what this was all about; now I was not so sure.

But yes, I believed in us. It was the very worst time of my life, and I didn't see how things could be any worse. I just knew that this would work out and that we would come through this to have an even stronger, closer relationship.

One morning upon returning from work, the phone rang. I had just climbed into bed, tired from the night shift, but I was up out of bed and into the living room as quickly as I could. There was a mixture of excitement and dread running through my body.

"Hello," I answered.

"Please don't hang up on me," it was Christine's voice on the other end of the line.

"I won't hang up," I assured her. If only she knew how I had waited for this call every day.

There was a pause, and then in a shaky, uncertain voice, Christine told me, "I have done something that you are not going to like, but it has made me realise how much I miss you, and I just want us to be back together. Can I come by and see you after I finish work today?" Christine asked.

"Yes, of course, you can," I assured her.

"Oh thank you," she continued. "I'll come by straight from work."

With that, my heart soared. Okay, it was obvious, Christine had been with another man, and no I didn't like it, but if that is what it took to bring us back together, well I would have to be grateful for that much at least. All of this ran through my head, and I was excited and hopeful while trying to get everything straight in my mind. Was there anything I should say, ask, do? How should we proceed to put this whole thing behind us, to sort things out so that we would never have to go through something like this again?

I lay there in bed, but it was soon obvious that I was not going to get any sleep that day. It didn't matter. What did I need to do? I got up and shaved, showered and got dressed. Normally for a work day, I would put on my old work clothes. Today I dressed up, I wanted to be looking nice.

I did a little bit of cleaning and tidying up, but there really was not a lot to do. Then I ate some lunch, and I waited. It was a long afternoon, but it didn't matter, it was worth waiting for. All of the pain and suffering was all about to fade away.

I waited for the phone to ring, announcing that Christine had arrived at the front door, but instead, there came a knock on my door. Someone had let her into the building. I rushed to the door, having rehearsed this moment a hundred times in my head.

My big moment, and I swung the door open. Christine barely glanced up at me as she sailed past and into the living room. I knew in an instant that everything was not all right.

"Is this okay?" she asked, sitting herself down on the sofa.

"Yes, sure, of course," I said, somewhat puzzled and concerned.

"I am sorry about this," Christine barely looked up at me. "I am sure you guessed, I had sex with somebody else last night for the first time, and well, I felt so bad about it this morning that I just wanted to be back with you. But now I don't," she continued.

What could I say? I asked myself, but there was nothing. Not in any of the scenarios that ran through my head that day had anything like this come up.

"I am really sorry," Christine said again, and then she was up, off of the sofa. "I have to go," and she was heading for the door.

I had always been sure this whole thing would work out, just as I had been sure that things could not get any worse. How wrong I could be!

125

I was devastated. I was in so much pain I could barely function. At work, I would break down in tears and have to find somewhere to hide. Back home in the morning and I would undress, climb into bed and cry myself to sleep. After that painful slap in the face, I didn't know how to cope.

I was even more lonely and lost, and there didn't seem to be a single ray of hope to hold on to. I tried the telephone dating service, just to have someone to talk to for a while. It was expensive and futile. I talked to one girl who told me that it was her birthday, that she was living with her brother and that he had not even acknowledged the fact.

We met up down the street from me. I told this stranger that I had wine at home or that we could go out somewhere for a drink. She told me that she didn't drink, but if I was willing to pay for it, she knew somewhere that she could buy some weed.

I hadn't smoked for years, and I didn't really want someone smoking in my place, but anything for some company. As it turned out, she bought something stronger, and my place didn't end up smelling of smoke. But it just wasn't my thing, and it ended up feeling worse than just being on my own. She was much younger and not unattractive, but her personality and the situation were just not right.

I tried to cope the best I could. Work, sleep, feed myself, repeat again tomorrow. I wasn't going out anywhere or doing anything else, and I began to notice at the end of the month that I still had money left over in my account. How could that be? We never had anything left over at the end of the month with two incomes. But there it was. If I could save up a deposit, I might be able to buy my own place.

I talked to my bank, and I started to pay into a retirement savings plan with the knowledge that I could withdraw the money to use as my deposit. It was going to take a couple of years, but at least there was something to be moving towards.

I was glad of the smallest bits of anything positive in my life. I forced myself to keep going to the camera club. I made myself get into the dark room and find a picture to print, something to enter into the monthly competition. Friends of ours, and friends of mine were there, occasional contacts, but they were never going to fill this void.

I noticed the bicycle was not hanging from Christine's balcony anymore. I never thought that I would say this, but I was glad that I had experienced severe depression when I felt trapped in the military as a teenager. If I had got through that, then I could do it again now.

I took life one day at a time. Sometimes it was one hour at a time, and at work in the middle of the night, not knowing where Christine was or even if she was safe, I would have to tell myself, just get through the next five minutes and then see how you feel.

126

Life was hard, and I had to force myself to function sometimes. But I still believed that we would get back together. We had a great relationship, and it wasn't just me. I had to hold on to that thought. That one little bit of hope!

It was six months since Christine left, and I hadn't heard

anything. I didn't know for sure where she was, I just had a vague feeling that she was somewhere to the east of me as I stared out at the sunrise every morning at work. I didn't know for sure, but I had the feeling that she had moved in with someone else, and that weighed heavy on my heart.

Suddenly, just after I had climbed into bed one morning, the phone rang. But I didn't rush to answer it this time. It could be anything, it could be anyone, I told myself, and then it stopped. Only to start again, a moment later. I have to answer that, I told myself, as this could be something serious.

"Hello," and I was answered by a voice I didn't recognise at first.

"This is Mrs Green, Christine's boss," she was telling me.

I feared the worse for a moment before she continued, "Christine would like to talk to you. Would you be willing to speak with her?" she asked.

"I can't," I was telling her. "I know what will happen."

"I understand," she said. "But I really think it will be different this time. There have been some changes in her."

I was scared. Christine was all I really wanted, but I was too afraid of what she could do to me after the last time.

"Oh, can you hold the line a moment please," Mrs Green was saying.

I thought that she had another call coming in on another line, or that someone had walked into her office, and I waited on the line.

"Hello, it's me." It was Christine's voice on the line. Her boss had just passed over the phone in the hopes that I wouldn't be rude enough to hang up on my wife.

"Hello Christine," I was trapped.

"Will you come and meet me?" Christine was asking. "I really want us to be back together, and I want us to get some counselling. Mrs Green is willing to refer us to this couples counsellor that she recommends."

"Okay, when do you want to get together?" I found myself asking Christine.

"As soon as you like really," Christine was saying. "Perhaps we could have lunch together. I am not going to be able to get any work done now," Christine added.

"I will be there by noon," I offered.

"That would be great! Oh, thank you, thank you," Christine said with an air of relief in her voice.

127

I showered and dressed with a mix of dread and subdued hope. Could this be real? Could it really be different this time as Mrs Green assured me? She is a psychologist after all, and her very involvement should be some comfort to me, and sure enough, she was there to greet me.

She took us both into her office and sat us down. "I want you to go off and have lunch together and talk about this," Mrs Green instructed us. "Take as long as you need, there is no rush, and when you get back here I want the two of you to tell me what you have decided, and we will take it from there. Then if this is what you want to do, I will give you a list of couples resources."

I was feeling more confident and more optimistic as we headed out of the office and across the street to find some lunch. The large Shoreside Hotel had a beautiful revolving restaurant, and we were early for what would be their busiest time of day. They showed us to a booth right by the window, we were looking out towards the North Shore at that time.

It was a bright sunny day, perfect for a new start as Christine began telling me what she was thinking. I listened intently, as I watched the tears that were forming in her eyes and rolling down her cheeks.

"This is really what I want to do," Christine was telling me. "I know that this has been hard for you, and I am sorry, but now I really want us to get back together. To get some help this time. To get some counselling."

The waiter arrived to take our orders, but it was immediately obvious that we had not even looked at the menus. "I'll give you some time," he said, and he was gone.

"I know that I am going to regret it for the rest of my life if I don't do this now," Christine told me. "Jenny, that's Mrs Green," Christine continued, "was telling me about a very successful couples retreat that they hold on Vancouver Island every couple of months. It is fairly expensive, but I think that it would be worth every penny."

"We could find the money," I offered.

"Then in the meantime, while we wait for that, she will give us a list of couples councellors that we can see. Your extended health care would cover much of that, wouldn't it?" Christine asked.

"We would just be paying a user fee," I confirmed.

I thought that I saw our waiter heading our way just as Christine reached across and grabbed both of my hands, but he never arrived. We sat while Christine talked, and I listened. The restaurant filled with people. I don't think there was an empty table left by the time our conversation had become less intense, and I noticed that we were almost back to our original view. It must have been one hour, one full revolution in this revolving room.

"Shall we go and let them have their table back?" Christine asked.

The waiter never even brought us a glass of water, but it was the best service I have ever received in any restaurant. I left him a tip on the table. It was the least I could do to say thank you.

128

As we left the hotel and stepped out into the sunlight, Christine took my hand. It felt right, it felt natural to be walking side by side, hand in hand, just as we had done for most of the past fifteen years. Then as we neared the office Christine stopped and leaned across to kiss me on the mouth.

I was feeling better about this by the minute. I knew that it was the right thing to be doing. I had no doubt that we belonged together. I heard all of the right things from Christine. Whereas an hour ago Christine was crying and looking down at her hands, now she was smiling and looking me in the eye.

So as we sat down in front of Mrs Green, I had hope for the first time in a long time.

"Okay, what have you two decided?" Mrs Green asked.

"We want to get back together," Christine stated. "We want to get counselling and sort this whole thing out."

"What about you?" Mrs Green looked my way.

"Yes, this is all I have ever wanted," I told her.

"Good," Mrs Green looked pleased. "Now do you have somewhere that you can stay tonight Christine? It would not be fair nor sensible to go straight back in together," she continued. "You both need a few days to sort yourselves out."

"I can go and ask Nancy." Christine sounded excited. She gave my hand a squeeze, and she dashed out into the next room to ask her co-worker.

Mrs Green was giving me a few words of encouragement while Christine was out of the room.

"Yes, I can stay the next couple of nights with Nancy and her husband," Christine explained. There was a bounce in her step as she came back into the room.

"Great," Mrs Green offered. "Now, have you told Nick that you are leaving him?"

"No," Christine admitted. "I will go and phone him right now."

"I really hope that this is going to work out for the two of you," Mrs Green sounded sincere.

"So do I," I confirmed, "so do I."

"Right, I suggest that you arrange to meet up, perhaps for dinner somewhere," Mrs Green was suggesting. "That will give you time to get home and pack a bag," she said, aimed at Christine. "Say six o'clock, will that work?"

"That would be great," Christine offered, "I know just the place."

"Then if that is okay with you," Mrs Green said, turning to me, "you can drive Christine over to Nancy's place."

"I will do that," I told them both.

129

By six o'clock, I sat with a menu in hand at the agreed upon restaurant. I was looking forward to this so much. Not this dinner with Christine, although we had pretty much skipped lunch, but being back together again.

The waitress came by and asked me if I wanted to order anything, but I assured her that I would wait for my guest. Then twenty minutes had passed, and no sign of Christine. I called the waitress over and ordered some coffee. My optimism was beginning to be challenged.

Another twenty minutes went by and not a word. The waitress refilled my coffee cup, and I began to realise that everything was not going to turn out as planned. I had been told that Christine was living just a short walk from this restaurant, I knew that she should easily have been here by now.

Just before seven, the restaurant phone was ringing. The waitress reappeared to tell me that Christine was sorry that she had been delayed, but she was on her way. I wanted to find some hope in that, but I had an uncomfortable feeling.

The restaurant door swung open, and Christine stepped in carrying a large red holdall. I could tell in an instant that it was empty. There was no weight pulling down on the handles as Christine held the thing away from her body so it didn't lose its shape. I am not sure why she brought it.

She reached down and touched my coat with an affectional pat. But she wasn't really looking at me as she dropped down into the chair across from me.

"I am sorry I kept you waiting," Christine started. "Nick and I had a long chat, and well, I've decided to stay with him."

"So what was today all about?" I asked. "What was all that about getting councelling?"

"I am sorry, I don't know, but I have told Nick that I wouldn't leave him." Christine was crying again. "He has been hurt before, you know."

"Did you eat already?" I asked.

"I have been snacking," Christine admitted. "I just wanted to pop over and let you know what I've decided."

"After all we said today. After all we talked about, what happened to that?" I continued, looking directly at her. I was at my wit's end.

"I should just get going and go home now," Christine was shaking and looking down at the tablecloth, running the material through her fingers. Anything to distract herself. She couldn't bring herself to look up at me.

"No, I want you to get in my car, and I am going to drop you off at Nancy's as arranged. They are expecting you, and you can sleep on it tonight. Make your decision tomorrow, that is the least you can do," I told her.

I already knew that it was futile, but I was determined not to just let her walk off into the night. We had told Nancy that she would be there, and Christine had not thought to phone her and let her know that she was not showing up. So I dropped her at Nancy's door, and I sat there and watched while she stepped inside.

Then I drove home alone in hopeless shock.

130

I had a great group of friends, without whom I would never have coped. My best mate apologised for telling me that I would be over Christine by now. In reality, my healing hadn't even begun at this point. But he took me downhill skiing on a regular basis. It is tough to be thinking of anything else while you are tumbling down the side of a mountain on a couple of planks of wood.

John would call me up out of the blue, and ask me if I had eaten yet. Very often this was just as I was about to start cooking. He would have some dish that he had wanted to try, and I was a willing guinea pig. We would share dinner with his wife, and then afterwards we would sit and talk. He would explain to me why he felt the need to upgrade his camera to the latest, just released version. He almost never used it to shoot pictures, but he could tell you every technical specification and why it was so much better than the previous one. His wife would be long gone at the mere mention of photography.

I would be invited to parties and camera club events, things that in previous years I had been to with Christine, but I made myself go. I was never great at mixing, but at least I knew some of the people, and that made it easier to talk. You didn't have to do anything other than listen when friends got their guitars out. I could have stayed in that moment forever.

But for the most part, I was home alone and finding it difficult to get through another day. I craved company but found it painful to be out on my own. I could only bring myself to go to the one pub where I knew my friend's son would be working. No matter how busy it was in there, he would always acknowledge my presence.

It wasn't a pickup bar as most of the clientele arrived as couples or in small groups. Seldom did I get to talk to anyone other than the bartender. I never let myself drink more than two pints of beer, although I would drag those pints out to last all night as I was reluctant to go home.

One night I was there having a hard time of it because it was coming up on the first anniversary of Christine leaving. I didn't want to be there, but I didn't want to be at home either. I really didn't want to be anywhere. I was sat on my usual barstool not far from the door, making my second pint last as long as I could, when this younger woman walked in.

She was obviously very drunk, and she started making a pass at anyone near the door. Any single male or any group of males drinking there were fair game. So I picked my drink up and started to move further along the bar. There was a woman more my age drinking on her own, and so I asked, "Would you mind if I sit here for a while? I really can't be dealing with her right now."

"Sure, go ahead," she told me with a smile, glancing down the far end of the bar.

I learned that this was her last night in town. She had been here for a convention, and that most of her colleges had already flown home. Her flight was not until early the next morning. She invited me back to her hotel room. I don't know why she asked me back there. Perhaps, she was craving company as much as I was.

We had sex. I was looking for a slow, gentle, romantic encounter, which finished abruptly when she said, "Haven't you finished yet?" We rolled over and fell asleep, to be woken at an early hour by her alarm clock.

Evenings out usually ended up making me feel worse than if I had stayed in, but there are only so many nights in a row you can stand to be home by yourself. I hadn't replaced the television, and perhaps I should have by now. I was working the graveyard shift and would be for a long time to come, and I found that I needed more hours of sleep to get through the nights.

But then there were my days off. I was getting to the lowest point of my life, and I was wondering how I could cope. Just get yourself through the next five minutes, and then see how you are doing, I would tell myself. Then five more, look, you managed the last five.

131

How Christine and I had been so short of money sometimes, I will never know. Okay, I didn't go anywhere anymore. I stayed in, paid my rent and my few bills, and I fed myself, that was it. Now twenty months after Christine left I was searching for an apartment, to buy. I had been pre-approved by the bank, and I was excited by the possibilities.

It had to have easy access to work. One single transit ride or better still, a short walk. It had to have some degree of privacy; I didn't want to be looking straight across at someone else's windows, and it had to be something that I could be proud of. Which was a tall order on a limited budget.

I searched around on my own, and I searched with the help of a realtor. I found what I thought would be the ideal place for me. A ground floor unit in a building that was yet to be finished. It had enough of a semi-private deck to have a barbeque and a table with four chairs. A loft, where you looked down from the bedroom into the living room, or through the tall floor to ceiling windows. Ideal, but it was sold.

That was my benchmark, and nowhere that I looked could quite measure up. Too far out of town, too old, too noisy or the area was wrong, and I was beginning to get frustrated with my search. I decided that I would go back to the building that I liked the most and settle for one of the higher floors without the nice outside deck. Then much to my surprise, the sale of my favourite unit had fallen through.

I was set. It would be another four months before the building was finished. Even then it was touch and go as to whether the move in date would happen in time. But I got there. My friends rallied around and helped move all of my things to a big pile in the middle of my new floor. The bed and the wardrobe had made it upstairs, but everything else was in the centre of the room.

Then I took my friends across the road for dinner as promised, but they wouldn't let me pay for anything. Not even my own meal. I was so grateful for the help and all the money that they had saved me. Then I was relieved not to be looking at the same four walls that Christine and I had shared for so many years. Yes, there would still be echoes of her here, but this was a place of my own.

I sat myself down on the top few stairs and surveyed my new home. Five hundred and sixty square feet for me to make of it what I will. Exciting possibilities, but first things first. I got my shower curtain up and my bathroom ready to use. Then I put my desk in the corner and fixed up my computer and internet connection.

My next most urgent item was curtains to cover my sixteen-foot windows. My place wasn't directly overlooked, but it wasn't totally private either. A mutual friend of Christine and mine had kindly offered to sew the curtains for me if I supplied the material. I was secretly pleased because I knew that Christine would get to hear the details of my new home. Even if I wasn't sure where she was living, she would know where I was.

Besides which, I had made sure to keep the same phone number, just in case. It had been eighteen months since that last disaster, but every time the phone rang, I couldn't help but think of Christine.

132

I didn't hear from her of course, I couldn't expect to. But every time the phone rang, it would be a telemarketer, a salesman or worse still, dead air. "Hello?" Nothing, not a sound. "Hello?" I would repeat in a gentler voice. If Christine did phone, she would likely be too scared to speak to me.

It wasn't realistic. I should have known better, but every call was a little moment of hope, and yet how would I dare to even try again after those last two times. So I took pride in my new place. I laid a parquet floor, found a beautiful linen rug, made the most of our old sofa and love seat.

John called me up. "Would you like our old television?" he asked. "We wouldn't get anything for it, so it is yours if you want it." They had just ordered a new set, and I was glad of it. I don't know how I had survived so long without one. Things were coming together. I had my music, and I had my computer, now with email and dial-up internet. But having television again was great.

One day as I arrived home from work, I picked up my mail. I dropped it on my kitchen counter while I put the kettle on, and then I looked to see who the bills were from. My pulse quickened. I couldn't understand what I was looking at. An envelope addressed to Christine from the local symphony orchestra.

Was it forwarded from our old address, no? It was Christine's full name, and it was my new address. I sat there looking at it. My mind was racing. How could this happen? Was it Christine just wanting to say hello? I smiled to myself. I had an ever-so-small degree of hope. I still believed in us, even though it had been more than two years at this point. But it should have worked out, I know it should have.

Then a couple of months later it was a letter from the Red Cross. Addressed to my address but with Christine's name on it. I didn't open any of the letters, I just collected them up and put them to one side. I was sure that this was just her way of saying 'hi'.

So the years passed and I collected a small pile of mail, all addressed to Christine at my new address. I didn't know what else to do with them. I couldn't throw them away, that would be a federal offence. I could have written 'return to sender' and dropped them back in the mail, but I doubted they would get back anywhere to be cancelled.

At first, I loved the fact that I was receiving mail for her, but after a couple of years, I just wanted to confront her about them. I knew that she had moved back closer to town, although I didn't have an address. However, I heard that she was teaching at a downtown adult training school. A bit of a surprise to me, I had no idea what she might be teaching.

However, I summoned up my courage and my resolve. I collected all of the mail into one large envelope with Christine's name on the front, and I headed in to drop it off. My pulse was racing, and I was feeling a little nervous.

Oh, she left here about a month ago, I was told when I asked for her at the front desk.

133

After more than four years on the graveyard shift, I started to get spells on the day shift. It wasn't permanent yet, that would take almost another year. But I was starting to feel more human again, and I did so much better on a decent night's sleep than I had trying to sleep during the day. Work was still work, but I was feeling healthier.

Then one day there was a dreadful accident. It wasn't one of the regular staff working indoors, but a contractor hired to do some work on the outside of the building. He had dismissed his workmate and was finishing up on his own at the end of the day. Instead of coming back down to ground level to move his lift-a-loft, he was adjusting its position from high in the air.

He drove one wheel off the curb, tipping the unit violently to the side and throwing him to his death. The police were there, the coroner, and the press filming the scene for the news broadcast that evening.

It was very subdued at work that day, even though we didn't know the young man. We had all taken our own shortcuts from time to time. We had all bent the safety rules. We even had similar machines indoors that we used occasionally. It gave us all pause for thought. Our weekly safety meetings were attended with a little more attention to what was being said for some time to come.

It was a long day with very little cheerful banter. There was only one subject of conversation, and by the time we left work that evening all signs of the incident had been removed. But I walked home still feeling a bit of shock from this event.

I turned on the news that evening to watch. It was the lead story and covered in detail with video from the film crew. The outside of our building was obvious, as were the results of the accident. But they hadn't released the young man's name at that point.

The evening's television helped to put the day's events out of my mind. Just the usual nonsense on the box, but a chance to relax and wind down before going to bed. I fell asleep without any difficulty.

But at ten minutes to three in the morning, I woke. I made my way downstairs to go to the bathroom. I was halfway across the room when the phone started ringing. I was there in about four quick steps.

"Hello." There was no answer, and I was sure in an instant that it was Christine on the other end of the line. "Hello," I repeated in a gentle tone, and I waited for a moment before I heard the click of a phone being hung up.

134

The months went by, and I hadn't heard anything more. But then one day I happened to be travelling through the local train station, and I saw Christine sitting on a bench, eating a sandwich. She didn't see me, she was just looking down at her lap, and the remains of the sandwich in her hand.

I debated in my mind whether to go over and say, 'hello'. Did I dare? Was I strong enough after all of these years? But I decided yes I could, at least, say hello. So I walked across towards her and all of this time her head was down staring into her lap, so she didn't see me walking up to her.

"Hi," I said as I stepped up in front of her. Her hands immediately came up in a defensive posture. One arm above her head and the other in front of her face. I was shocked by her reaction. I had never seen her so scared.

"I am not going to hurt you," I said as her arms dropped back to her lap. "I just wanted to say hello," I added. But she was shrinking back into herself like a cornered mouse that thought it was about to be consumed.

She couldn't speak; she couldn't even look up at me, and all I wanted to do was to wrap her up in a warm, secure hug and let her know that she was safe now. But all I could do was to turn and walk away, devastated and frightened for her. What could have brought her to this point?

Now that I knew that Christine might be there I would go out of my way to be in that area. I would sit and pour over a coffee in the station cafe. I would walk through the station in one direction and then circle around and walk back the other way. Though for much of the time, there was no sign of her.

When I did see her, she had her head down staring into a

half-eaten sandwich in her lap, and I didn't want to frighten her or cause her any stress. So I would quietly walk by and head for home, content to know that she was there.

Then one day I was walking home from work on my usual route, I was finally full-time day shift. Christine was sitting at a desk in the window of what I could only describe as a cult church. She was looking out of the window and watching me walk down the road.

After which, I would look across and look straight at her, time after time on my way home from work, and I didn't know what to make of her watching me. But oh, how I wanted her to just get up from her desk and step outside of that door. Then I could stop, walk up to her, say something. But she stayed rooted to her desk.

I continued to visit the railway station. I knew by now that Christine would arrive there on the local sea bus, and so I would stand outside of the station at weekends, watching for the Seabus to arrive and then walk into the station as the passengers poured out towards the street. No sign of Christine. Then I would go back out again and watch over the fence for the next Seabus to arrive.

135

It wasn't quite the digital age of photography yet, but you could scan your film into a digital file, and I had started to work on pictures on my computer. I had one of the very early programs for processing pictures, and I was eager to learn how to use it.

I had a beautiful photograph of Christine, and I had the sentimental words from one of my favourite songs. It took about thirty-six hours of work, of trial and error, but I combined the words and the picture on a single page. You could start reading from the top of the page, and as you reached the top of Christine's head, the words faded out only to continue again at the bottom of the page.

I framed it in a really lovely gold frame, and I carried it with me, time after time, until I saw Christine sitting in the station one evening. I walked up to her sitting there with her sandwich, and there was no defensive reaction this time. So I told her about it, and that I just wanted her to have it. She seemed secretly pleased and graciously accepted it. I was relieved. I just wanted her to know that I still cared, even after all of this time.

If I had hoped that this would be enough to get her to step out of that door as I walked by, or to pick up the phone and call me, nothing happened. She would still sit there and follow me with her eyes as I walked home from work, and I would still glance across at her, willing her to step out of that door. 'Stand up from your desk and take the four or so steps to the front door.' I tried sending her that message.

It never happened. I had promised the psychologist that I would never be the one to initiate contact, but we had been in contact, and I still had this growing pile of mail addressed to her. So I gathered it all again into a big brown envelope and wrote her name on the outside.

I took it with me, and I walked through that door and up to the desk where I had seen her so many times. Christine was not there, but there was a girl I had never seen before walking by. "Is Christine here?" I asked. "I have some mail for her."

"No, she finished here two days ago," she told me.

"Oh, do you have a forwarding address for her?" I asked. "I have this mail I wanted to get to her."

"We have no idea where she has gone," this aggressive male voice announced from somewhere at the back of the room. He sounded angry.

So for a second time, I had missed my chance to give her this pile of mail. That was it. Every evening when I walked home, I watched for her, but she was never at the desk in front of the window.

I continued to arrive at the railway station. I continued to stand outside and watch for the ferry to arrive, and then I would skip around to the front door to watch the people arriving. There was no sign of her anymore.

I had a sense of where she lived, but I didn't have an address. Besides which, I would never just show up there even if I knew. But she wasn't there anymore, no matter how many cups of coffee I sat there and drank, dragging them out until they were cold.

Then, when I had given up on seeing her at the station, I was walking by on my way to do some shopping. Suddenly she was there in front of me. She threw her arms around my neck and hugged me tight to her body. She was sobbing on my shoulder, and I was hugging her back.

She just held onto me, and I could feel her tears rolling down my cheek. She pulled away, and I could see the tears on her face. "I am sorry," she told me. And then she started talking at a hundred miles an hour. She barely stopped for breath. I had never heard her talk so fast.

"I was stuck in there working for those people for nothing, and they just expected more and more, they were not going to let me go and I was trapped, but my then boyfriend marched in there and told them that I was gone and if they did anything to try to hold on to me or chase me down, he would slap them with a lawsuit, faster than that, but he was abusive and controlling and he kept putting me down. Luckily my parents had arrived from England, and my mother was there and saw what he was doing to me, he was abusive to me right in front of her, and she said that was it, and she made me collect all of my things, and she marched me out of the door. Thank God for her, because I had no backbone left, I couldn't stand up for myself, I had nothing left, I wasn't myself anymore. I am sorry," she paused for breath.

Then out of the corner of her eye, she saw a car pulling up across the road. "I am sorry, that is my ride," she told me. I had no idea who was picking her up, who was in the car, but she stepped back away from me. There was no goodbye hug, and I didn't look across at the car, I just let her go.

She was talking to me, and I felt that I had somehow left the door open for her to call me up. I had not been angry, and I was not judgemental. I was open to what she had to say, and she seemed to want to talk to me, to explain what was happening in her life.

I did my shopping, and I went home happy, feeling sure that I would hear more. But the weeks went by and nothing. I had always had a sense of where Christine was. Whether it was looking out at the sunrise while I was working graveyard, or more recently feeling that she was there somewhere to the north of me, and then one day I had the sense that she wasn't there anymore.

I began to feel that she was somewhere far off to the east of me. Eastern Canada, maybe, or back in England. It would be years before I would hear for sure.

Epilogue

Fourteen years had gone by, and although I had promised myself countless times, 'by this time next year, I will be in a new relationship', it hadn't happened. Perhaps I was expecting too much. Perhaps I had set my sights too high. Or maybe I feared that as I had no idea what had happened to end this relationship, it would be my destiny to suffer the same painful feat again.

So, I was still single. No closer to having someone new in my life than I was the day Christine left. But I was making the most of what I had. Enjoying the new home I had created for myself. Enjoying the company of some new friends and my old friends too.

Of course, I continued with my photography, getting more involved with my camera club. Moving from my favourite position hiding at the back of the club, to standing in front, leading meetings. First as print chair, then as Vice President and President.

I continued to win awards, even had some of my portraits published in a national magazine, and I was more than a little grateful to find that models Christine had found for me were still willing to come along and pose. Happily, several of them had become long-term friends. As far as I knew, Christine had not stayed in touch with anyone we had known.

It was a long weekend mid-summer, and I went to visit my half-brother in the Okanagan. Sunshine, barbeque, and glasses of wine out on his patio. Just pure relaxation and family time. Then, of course, I had taken my laptop with me, and I checked my email from time to time.

There was an email from Christine. We didn't have email when she had left me, and we hadn't been in touch, in all these years. So, either she had contacted a mutual friend, or she had searched me out on the internet. One way or the other, I was sat there looking at her email message.

It read, 'I hope you are well and that you don't mind me asking, but do you still have a copy of our divorce papers? I never picked mine up, and now I am planning to get married again, and well, I need them.'

I gave myself a day to think about it and let it sink in before I wrote back. 'Hi Christine, it is a long weekend, and I am at my brother's place, but as soon as I get back home tomorrow evening, I will have a look through my paperwork.'

By the time I had arrived back in Vancouver I had a second email. 'Thanks, but I have managed to get in touch with the old law firm I used to work for, and they are going to pick up my copy, and send it to me.'

I had the distinct feeling that she just wanted to share the information with me, and perhaps to be in touch again. I had, over the years, come to an interesting conclusion which I will share with you presently.

We stayed in touch via email after that. I learnt they had not known each other very long, and I wondered at the wisdom of this rush to marry, but I didn't comment. In fact, I restricted my correspondence to birthday wishes and Christmas greetings, for the most part.

I was pleased to know she was safe and healthy and that she had a good job which she enjoyed. Then I told myself, 'give your head a shake.' I had already started to ask myself questions about my retirement. Where was I going to live? What was I going to do with myself? But every question led me to the thought, I was going to want to have someone in my life, someone to share my time with.

So far, I had been singularly unsuccessful in my attempts to meet someone, but perhaps it was just that the time was right. By sheer dumb luck or coincidence, I met a lovely lady who shared many of my interests. My taste in music, my enjoyment of live theatre, and of dance.

We dated for a while, then a few overnight stays became a more permanent sharing of an apartment. Later we married and searched ourselves out a place to retire to in the Okanagan. A lovely detached house on a hillside. We planted fruit trees, and made ourselves planter boxes to grow some of our own vegetables.

What a lovely place to live, summer and winter! Lakes and parks and outdoor events in the summer. Live theatre, music, dance and a ski hill a short drive away in the winter. I loved the area, but the area didn't love me it seemed.

Over time my sinuses became obstructed, and I had a lot of congestion in my lungs. I was referred to an ears, nose and throat specialist and to a lung specialist. I had CT scans and various medical remedies, but it got to the point where I was waking four or five times a night and having to go and sit out in the lounge, trying to clear my nose.

My ENT specialist referred me to another ENT specialist and then another one after that, and finally, I was put on the waiting list for a sinus operation. But it was going to be months away, and in the meantime, I was left to suffer.

However, we had already booked ourselves a Baltic cruise, followed by two months in England with my family. I did wonder how I would cope, and I worried, would I be waking the household up every night with my cough? But I was determined to go and to enjoy the trip the best I could.

We flew to London and then on to Copenhagen. What a beautiful city! Two days to explore there, and a chance to meet up with friends. Then it was off on our cruise. I need not have worried about how I would do. Within three or four days of our cruise starting, I was breathing through my nose and sleeping through the night.

By the time we reached England, I was feeling great. There was a spring in my step that hadn't been there while I was waking so many times in the night. Before the two months were up touring England and staying with my sister, I had another pleasant surprise. I walked into my sister's kitchen one evening towards the end of our stay, and I could smell food cooking.

Back home again in the Okanagan and I was going downhill, just as fast as I had recovered. My doctor suggested I go and live on a cruise ship, and then he sent me to see an allergy specialist. It turned out I was allergic to so much of the local vegetation. Wild grasses, trees, fungi that lived in the trees and soil amongst other things.

I was beginning to think I should be living in England, but I decided to try a few other options first. I had the chance to house sit on the West Coast for three weeks, and I took it. I wasn't getting any worse, but I wasn't getting any better either. Then I took a short-term rental north of the Okanagan Valley. A different microclimate, but I didn't get the sort of benefits I had enjoyed in Europe.

So my wife very graciously told me she would release me, and leave me free to move to England. She didn't want to move so far away from the rest of her family, but if it meant me getting my health back and not having to face an operation, then that is what I should do.

I had had the same operation once before. It wasn't a cure, but it had given me a better quality of life for about ten years. However, if I could avoid having an operation and get my health back, then I felt it was the thing to do.

Reluctantly I sold a lot of things that were dear to me: my downhill skis, my studio lights and other photographic props, things I couldn't take to England. Many other items I didn't sell, non-essential household items that my wife might be able to make some use of.

Then we went into a lawyers office and filed for a mutually-agreed divorce. I think it was a first for them, two people happily filing for divorce together, and splitting the bill fifty-fifty. But there was no animosity, and I was so grateful for her help and support. She had been there and seen the dramatic improvement I had enjoyed on our Europe trip, and honestly, I would never have coped without her support.

I had let my family know of my intention to move back to England. All of my sisters lived in the West Country, a pleasant but quiet area. No real dance studio, only occasional live theatre and not much by way of an active photographic group.

I had also let Christine know that I was moving back, and I asked her if she would help me find a flat. She was living less than an hour out of London, and I knew there would be a lot more to hold my interest it that area.

"Why don't you come and stay with me?' Christine emailed back. 'We both know that is where we want to end up.'

I had an instant dread, a premonition almost, this was not the best idea, but how could I say no. I had never stopped believing that our relationship should have worked out. We had hit it off on my brief visit with her the last time I was in England. However, I had thought to find a flat nearby, see her from time to time and see what happened.

Now suddenly I was there with her. There was a huge amount of affection between us. We cuddled on the sofa. We walked everywhere hand in hand, and we talked. Christine had cleared out one-quarter of her wardrobe for me and bought a set of drawers. I could easily have filled half the wardrobe and half of all of the drawer space, but I squeezed in as best I could.

What would you like to see happening? Where do you see yourself, where do you see us, in five years' time? Christine was younger and really enjoyed her work, but I could see myself as a house husband. I was ready to jump back into a relationship and sail off into the sunset, as it were.

I learned that she was having an affair with someone she used to work with, and who had been very supportive of her. Someone she now considered her best friend. Christine didn't get to see him very often, but I had to tell her, I was not prepared to share her with another man.

So, the affection continued, and it was very genuine. I craved that affection and the closeness we used to share. I was there with her now, and my things had arrived from Canada, perhaps things can still work out.

We continued to talk. We talked about what had happened, and the breakup. Finally, after all of these years, I was about to get some closure.

She told me how the psychologist we were seeing had told her, 'A short, sharp breakup would be kinder to me in the long term. Be definitive, don't give out mixed messages.'

I told her how that same psychologist had made me promise not to, 'try to get her back.' "He said he was worried about you, and that any pressure from me might be a disaster. He was worried about what you might do to yourself."

"Oh, and I thought you weren't interested anymore," Christine was telling me.

"All of the time you were living in that abusive relationship, I was just living at home waiting for a call from you," I told her.

We stood in Christine's kitchen, and we cried. We held each other tight, and we sobbed. Historical misconceptions that were still raw. Misunderstandings, miscommunications, but now for me at least some understanding of what had been happening all those years ago.

"I love you so much," Christine told me.

"And I you," I answered.

I somehow remained optimistic, although there in the

back of my mind was the realisation Christine was having an affair with someone.

2

Then one day I received a phone call from Christine.

"I am on my way home," Christine announced. My father has taken ill and has been rushed to the hospital. I need to be there as soon as I can," she continued.

"I will go and rent a car right now," I told her. "I'll be ready to go by the time you get here. Do you have any details?" I asked.

"I am just getting on the train right now," Christine told me. "I will fill you in when I get home."

As quickly as we could, we were in the car and heading west, towards London. I had no idea of the route at this stage, and I missed our turn, so we just kept going. The straightest route, right through London. Christine had never learned to drive, but she did have a good idea of her way around London. Rush hour was over, and we just kept pushing on, but it was at least four hours to the West Country and the hospital where her father had been taken.

When we got there Christine's father was conscious and propped up in bed, her mother was sitting next to the bed holding his hand.

"Oh Chrissy, thank you for getting here so soon," Christine's mother was saying, as she got up from her chair to give her daughter a hug. "And thank you, for getting her here," she added with a quick smile in my direction.

It was twenty-five years since I had seen either of them, but I would soon feel that they were genuinely pleased to see me back in Christine's life.

"How are you doing Dad?" Christine was asking, with tears in her eyes, and concern in her voice.

"I'm doing good," her father replied in his chipper fashion, reaching up to give his daughter a hug.

"So, what has happened?" Christine was asking.

"I have lost all feeling and function in my lower body," her father offered in a matter-of-fact way.

"He is lucky to still be with us love," her mother was saying to Christine. "It usually kills most folk, on the spot."

We were trapped in this surreal world. Trapped between hope and despair. Christine slept in the double bed with her mother. I was sleeping on the chair that pulled out to a single bed in the lounge. After breakfast in the morning, we were back at the hospital to sit around her father's bed. Making small talk and awaiting test results.

Then it was Sunday afternoon, and Christine had to be back at work on Monday morning.

"I love you, daddy," Christine assured her father with a prolonged hug.

We were on the road again, totally unsure of the prognosis. Not knowing whether we might be dashing back again any time soon. Mr Wilson was sent home soon afterwards.

The dining room table was replaced with a hospital bed. The community nurses were organized for a daily visit. Bed baths and blood pressure monitoring and dishing out the medication. Then Mrs Wilson was left to cope with the rest, and her husband was not the ideal patient.

They also installed a hoist above Mr Wilson's bed and another above his favourite chair in the lounge. But Christine's father was in no mood to help himself. Mrs Wilson managed to get him out of bed and into a wheelchair a couple of times, but without any gratitude or help from her husband, she soon realised it was a wasted effort.

I knew that this would not be our last urgent trip west to Christine's parents' place, or to a hospital ward, and so I went out and bought a car. Happily, the quality of used vehicles at a reasonable price was considerably better than the last time I owned a car in England.

Finding a mid-size five-door Ford with a brief warranty period from a local garage gave me a reasonable degree of confidence. But I immediately joined the AA just to be on the safe side. This was England, you take a wrong turn and all of a sudden you are a mile or more out of your way. So, I went out and bought the Sat-Nav system. I wasn't planning on missing my turns and ending up driving through the middle of London again.

Christine was torn in two. After a long week at work, she just wanted a chance to relax, wind down and enjoy her home and garden. But she also felt duty bound to be there for her parents. So, every three or four weeks, straight after work on Friday evening I would drive her the four hours west so we could be with them.

We soon found it essential to book ourselves into a hotel room for each visit. Christine's mother would want to be in bed by eight o'clock at the very latest. She would likely be up during the night, and she would be up very early in the morning for sure. At least at the hotel, we could wind down and relax in the evenings and have a decent breakfast at a time that suited us, before spending the rest of the day visiting.

Mr Wilson wasn't improving any, nor did he seem to be getting any worse, despite the realisation that sometimes he would spit out his medication. How he expected those pills to disappear, I'll never know, because there they were at his next bed bath, or the next time they changed his bedding. He would play with his food some days, and generally give the appearance of a spoiled little boy, much to the frustration of his wife, who was doing her utmost to be as supportive as she could be.

So, we were certain Christine's father would never recover. But what we had no way of knowing was whether he had hours, days, weeks, or months to live. We had promised ourselves a holiday together, somewhere sunnier and warmer, but we didn't feel that we could fly off taking the chance of having to rush back at a moment's notice. Booking return tickets if we had to cut our trip short would be difficult and expensive.

Instead, we took a train to the South of France. Charging through the Channel Tunnel at breakneck speed. You barely realised that you were underground before you were popping out the other side. We managed to relax some, knowing we could be back again within a day if we had to. French food, the countryside, the architecture and the Roman ruins provided just the break we needed.

There was some sunshine and enough warmth to sit out in the street-side cafes, but not enough to lay on the beach, nor enough to tempt us to dip our toes in the Mediterranean, but it was a delightful place to just be. Soon we were back on the train and heading home. We reached Paris with just enough time to catch a taxi from one train station to another. Not my dream trip to the 'City of Lights'. We passed through with hardly a chance to even realise where we were.

Then we were home, and Christine's father was still stable. Every few weeks we made our dutiful trip to his bedside. Mrs Wilson's husband had always suggested that she wasn't safe to be crossing the road on her own with her limited eyesight, but she was doing perfectly well. Crossing the road safely and getting the shopping in, doing the household chores, and generally looking after her husband.

It was many months and many visits later when Christine's father passed away in his sleep one night. We got the long-expected phone call early one morning, and very soon we were headed west again. This time to an empty bed, the making of funeral arrangements, and the visits from friends and neighbours.

We arranged to go and see him laid out in his coffin. The

three of us stood there, each getting our own personal closure, and then there were a subdued few days before the service and the cremation.

"Would you mind if Trevor comes to the funeral service?" Christine was asking me. "I would like to have him there for support."

There was no way that I could say no to her request. I had met Trevor a few times before at events we had attended, and I knew they had seen each other on a very occasional basis. These were Christine's dark hours after all, and she deserved all of the comforts she could get. Christine had been there for me when my own mother had passed many years before.

So, Trevor arrived at the house the night before the funeral. He had never met either of the Wilsons before, but he swept in and wrapped Mrs Wilson up in his arms, expressing his deepest sympathy. He was like the prodigal son that had reappeared out of nowhere.

The following morning, he arrived back at the house, and I drove the four of us to the crematorium, where I was relegated to the sidelines. Christine sat on the front pew holding hands with her mother on her left and Trevor on her right. I was sat to Trevor's right, wondering about the surreal situation I was finding myself in.

3

Naturally, things were very subdued back at Christine's place for the next weeks and months. We were both dreading that first trip back to see Christine's mother. She had always been very difficult to deal with, and now we thought she might just collapse in on herself and give up on life.

We were both feeling duty bound to make that visit, and Christine was on the phone to her mum nearly every day. We were going to have to make the trip soon, but then I fell and broke my leg. There was no way that I could drive for the next six weeks at least. I wasn't even going to be able to cope with public transport.

Mrs Wilson understood. She was glad of the support that she was still getting from neighbours. She was happy that Christine still thought to call every day. She was doing all right under the circumstances.

By the time we made that first trip, we were pleasantly surprised. We had grown used to being told that we were doing this thing or that thing wrong. We were used to her mother snapping "Chrissy really," and levelling some degree of blame for something her daughter had done or not done.

But the visit went off without any animosity, and the next visit even more so. Mrs Wilson had joined the local church group, and she was picked up and driven to events within the group. She had also joined a craft circle, they met up nearby on a regular basis. Besides which, the neighbours still looked in on her or invited her over for tea. She had a social life, she was free to plan her own days for perhaps the first time in her adult life.

However, back at Christine's flat things were changing. I had hoped that the passing of her father would release her from her past and allow her to deal with the pain and confusion of her childhood. I had thought that we might enjoy a renewed closeness. Instead, Christine started to push me away.

Most of her workweek resulted in ten-hour days. Eight hours of work and two of travelling. I put the vacuum around, did the laundry, dropped off Christine's business attire at the dry cleaners. I did the grocery shopping and cooked an evening meal.

On the weekend we would go shopping together, except Christine would go marching off in front of me. No longer holding hands nor even walking beside me; I was still having trouble with my leg. We sat on the settee watching television. No longer cuddled up together, now we sat at opposite ends, and Christine snapped at me if I got too close to the middle of the sofa.

I moved into the back bedroom and slept on the pull-out chair that was little more than a mattress on the floor, and there I cried my last tears for a love that should have been. I could have moved out, but I knew no one else in that area. I could have moved to the West Country, but my sisters were wrapped up in their own lives. My childhood friends had long since moved on.

So, I decided to move back home to Canada. The one place where I still had friends I knew would be glad to see me. I shipped my things back, I sold my car, and I booked my ticket. I would have stayed forever for half of the affection we once enjoyed.

I went and picked up the dry cleaning, and the girl there told me how lucky Christine was to have a father like me. And I wondered, was that all I ever was to Christine? Was I the surrogate father that gave her a more acceptable second childhood? Was that what our fifteen years together was?

We stood in the kitchen the night before my flight, and Christine told me, "I love you so much. I am sorry I have never dealt with my stuff."

I told her, "I love you too," then there was a long hug and painful tears.

Christine was up in the morning and gone for her usual seven o'clock train. I showered, dressed, and packed my last few things. I fed the goldfish, and I made a fuss of the cat, then I placed the key on the bottom step, and let myself out of the door.

Colin MacArthur was born in Canada but has lived nearly half of his life in the U.K., he has always had an interest in writing and the written word. He has been published as a photographer and had one-man exhibitions of his photographs both in his home country and in England. He feels strongly that sharing his experience might help others cope, if they find themselves in similar circumstances.

Contact info:

Colin MacArthur
www.colinmacarthur.ca
colin@colinmacarthur.ca